HAUNTED BARS & PUBS OF MICHIGAN

NICOLE BEAUCHAMP

Published by Haunted America
A Division of The History Press
Charleston, SC
www.historypress.com

Front and back cover photos copyright of Amy Shabluk.

First published 2023

Manufactured in the United States

ISBN 9781467154307

Library of Congress Control Number: 2023934792

This book is dedicated to my parents, Ellen and Harold Beauchamp, for always being present for my events and successes, and to my brother, Bruce Beauchamp, for being the biggest inspiration in my life. I would not be where I am today if not for you.

I love you all so much!

CONTENTS

Preface   7

Acknowledgements   11

Mystery and Merlot: The Agitated Grape Bar & Bistro   15

Tequila with a Side of Terror: Fiesta Mexicana
        Restaurant & Cantina   22

Two Martinis with a Shot of Misogyny: Marley's
        Bar & Grill   29

East Coast Scare: The Side Door Saloon at
        The Blue Pelican Inn & Restaurant   37

Spirits, Skulls and Cider: The C-Pub and Fourth Coast
        Ciderworks at Canterbury Village   44

Wraiths of the Red Light: Clive & Dot's Anchor Inn   53

Familial Phantoms: Abick's Bar   61

Graveyard Mayhem at the Grotto: Dexter Beer Grotto   70

Brewed to the Bitter End: Jamesport Brewing Company   77

The Apple Doesn't Fall Far from the Scream: Robinette's
        Apple Haus & Winery   83

Ale, Apparitions, Attachments and Antiques: 7 Monks Taproom
        and Low Bar   88

Contents

Absolut-ely Eerie: Holden Green Tavern   95

Specters of the Soo: The Palace Restaurant & Saloon   100

Walter the Wanderer: Thirsty Llama Pub N Grub   107

Sláinte Among the Spooks: Coonan's Irish Hub   113

Bibliography   119
About the Author   127

PREFACE

On July 14, 2022, I visited what many believe to be the most haunted pub in the entire world: The Red Lion in Avebury, Wiltshire, United Kingdom. Formerly an old farmhouse, it is the only pub across the globe that sits within a more than four-thousand-year-old ancient stone circle. After entering and placing my order with the bartender, I sat down to enjoy my pint. As I carefully sipped the overflowing glass of hard apple cider, I couldn't help but notice that everyone seemed interested in a table in the room just ahead of me. There was a family dining at it, and I felt uncomfortable at the thought of disturbing them. In the end, curiosity got the best of me. After a few more sips of my cider to calm my nerves and gather up some courage to investigate further, I stealthily made my way to the other room and hastily peeked at the table where the family were sitting. I soon learned that it wasn't really a table at all. It was an eighty-six-foot-deep well from the 1600s that had been incorporated into the interior of the pub during an expansion project and now had a piece of glass resting atop it. Historically, the well has a macabre past.

While ghost sightings are rife at The Red Lion and include a few cowering children, a female writer, a farmer holding a knife and a horse-drawn carriage that, if spotted barreling through the courtyard, is an augury of death, the spirit that is most commonly seen is that of a woman called Florrie. Florrie married young and, after the wedding, barely saw her husband, as he went to fight in the English Civil War. In a moment of bitter loneliness, Florrie

The Red Lion in Avebury, Wiltshire, United Kingdom. *Author's photo.*

allowed herself to become intimate with another man. She believed that her husband would never find out about the affair, but one day he came home unexpectedly. In a fit of rage, he murdered her lover and then slit her throat. He then dragged her body to the lengthy well and dropped her in, later covering the opening with a boulder.

These days, she is spotted around The Red Lion wearing a dark floor-length dress with a cinched waist and long sleeves, while her chocolate-brown hair cascades down her shoulders. The pub experiences everything

Avebury Henge and Stone Circle. *Liz Cormell.*

from full-bodied apparitions to electrical issues to poltergeist activity. But the most frightening experience of all? Florrie has been seen on multiple occasions crawling in and out of the well. It is said that she doesn't like men with beards, as they remind her of her murderous husband, and will come after visitors with facial hair. Thankfully, I had nothing to worry about while I was there.

It appears that all the employees there have their own personal ghost stories. While visiting there was truly fascinating, it also got me thinking—how many watering holes in my home state of Michigan are haunted? I knew about Old City Hall in Bay City and The Whitney's Ghost Bar in Detroit, as I wrote about them in my last two publications, *Haunted Bay City, Michigan* and *Haunted Detroit*, but I wanted to learn more.

Once I began my research, I quickly learned some mind-blowing statistics about Michigan's level of alcohol consumption. If you can believe it, the average Michigander drinks a whopping twenty-three gallons of alcohol every year, and in my home county of Bay County alone there are approximately eighty-nine drinking establishments. It's no surprise that Michigan loves to drink. I knew I had my work cut out for me when I took on this project to find some of the most haunted bars and pubs across the state of Michigan, but I also knew that I wouldn't have to look far.

If you're feeling adventurous, go ahead and take a shot every time I use the word *paranormal* in this book. On second thought, maybe don't, because something tells me you'll be up to twenty-three gallons in no time, and I will not be held liable for any shenanigans that ensue after that!

ACKNOWLEDGEMENTS

A huge thank-you to John Rodrigue from The History Press for allowing me this amazing opportunity. To my late grandparents, Alfred and Evelyn Perry, for leaving such a positive impact on my life. To my mother, Ellen; father, Harold; brother, Bruce; my Aunt Amy, Aunt Irina, Uncle Rex, Uncle Mike; and cousins Perry, Lauren, Alex, Sasha and Maria for being an incredible family. To Kati Jones, Stephanie Gatza, Frances Kermeen, Michelle Jean Blankenship, Kayleigh Pantling, Angel Hartford-Porter, Micheala Cowdrey, Liz Cormell and Carrie and Reanna Crowl for believing in me even when I didn't believe in myself. To Bobby Jereb and Amy Shabluk (Portraits by Amy Michelle) for not only being incredibly supportive friends to me but also for being two of the most talented (and beautiful!) women I know. This project would not be what it is without you!

Thanks to the owners, staff and volunteers from the locations I wrote about that assisted me in getting content: Angela Hudson and Cindy Facknitz of The Agitated Grape; Terry and David Ranshaw of Fiesta Mexicana Restaurant & Cantina (formerly The Stockyard BBQ and Brew); Mary Lou Hoffman of Marley's Bar & Grill; Trisha Poirier and Christopher Corbett of The Blue Pelican Inn; Amanda and Terri Sharp of Down the Rabbit Hole, Cindy Sayre of Revival Salon/C-Pub and Jason Womack, all of Canterbury Village; Ronda and Jason Spears of Clive & Dot's Anchor Inn; Eric Lakeman, Kit Lindamood and Jessica Trail of Abick's Bar; Phil Blass and Phil Mekas of the Dexter Beer Grotto; Jennifer Tooman of

Jamesport Brewing Company; Kerrie Van Eck, Kare Greenup, Beverly West and Alicia Robinette of Robinette's Apple Haus & Winery; Jim Smolak and Laura Allore of 7 Monks Taproom/Low Bar; Steve and Schelley Schroeder and Sarah Calkusic of Holden Green Tavern; Tammy Cook of The Palace Restaurant & Saloon; Terry Bonnau, Jay Burnett and Monica Chambers of Thirsty Llama Pub N Grub; and Sheryl and Kim Coonan, Erin Coonan-Whisman and Trisha Pergande of Coonan's Irish Hub.

To the individuals and paranormal teams who shared ghost stories and content with me, including Marc Ortiz of Haunt Investigators of Michigan, Erin Schaefer, Jen DeGregorio, Rachael Schulz and Brian Danhausen. To the historians, archive collectors, educational faculty and organizations, photographers and friends who provided me with helpful information and abundant resources for the book: Jamie Kramer of the Bay County Historical Society; Kate Van Auken of the White Pine Library Cooperative; Patti Dawson of Central Lake District Library; Kurt Augustine, Michelle Aniol and Chloe Graham of the City of Dexter; Janet O'Keefe of the Flint Public Library; Sherry Copenhaver of the Courthouse Square Museum; Larry and Rebecca Peterson of the Schoolcraft County Historical Society; Tonya Cole of Washtenaw County; Paul Heidbreder of the *Traverse City Record-Eagle*; Alice Cruz and Beth Sheridan of the Orion Township Public Library; Mark and Sharon Konieczny of the Orion Historical Society; Nancy Van Blaricum of the Dexter Area Historical Society; Mike Gillis of MLive License; Karen Gonyea of the Manistique School and Public Library; Jeremy Dimick of the Detroit Historical Society; John Preville of the Bayliss Public Library; Carla Reczek of the Detroit Public Library; Sheila Bissonnette of the Pere Marquette District Library; Jim Orr of the Collections of The Henry Ford; Jennifer Andrew of the Grand Rapids History Center at the Grand Rapids Public Library; Houghton Lake Public Library; Allen Funeral Home of Davison; Alice and Jack Wirt Public Library; Sault Ste. Marie Public Library; Sherman Township Library; the City of Bay City; and Kelly and Fred Hinkson, Brian and Bridgett Beckwith, Rob Kokko, Katie Benghauser, Kera Statuch, Kate Way and Liz Cormell and Michelle Jean Blankenship (again!).

I want to give a heartfelt thanks to my supporters, social media followers, extended family and online friends who have watched me continue to grow and blossom over the last fourteen years. My journey has been a long one and at times rather grueling, so I want to recognize you guys for believing in me and continuing to be there for me even when the going got tough. I could never have done this without you all, and I can't stress enough how much I want you all to know that. Your constant love means everything to me and keeps me going. Shout out to my self-proclaimed no. 1 fan, Allison Baker. Stay sweet always! I adore you!

Mystery and Merlot

The Agitated Grape Bar & Bistro

310 North Main Street
Davison, MI 48423

Paranormal researchers usually find that the lingering energy that is contributing to a haunting seems isolated to the structure or property itself, but that energy can also be attached to objects and even people. When that happens, it's referred to as an "attachment" and can be either benevolent or malevolent in nature. It was a sunny spring day in May 2017 when Angela and John Hudson decided to clean out their recently leased property at 310 North Main Street in Davison, which has been long believed by local historians to be the second-oldest building in the city, having been erected in 1882. While throwing a bag of junk into the dumpster, John noticed a tiny porcelain hand sticking up among other garbage on the ground leftover by the previous owner. *What is this?*, John thought to himself as he reached for the little hand, pulling it out from beneath the debris. Brushing off the dirt, he could see that the doll was designed after the likes of an Irishman, with its curly red hair and beard, long kelly-green stockings and a shamrock pinned to its vest. John immediately brought it inside to show Angela. "Hey, check this out. Look what was lying next to the dumpster!" Angela looked at her husband with hesitation. "John, I think we should just throw that out. There's a reason it's out there." John shook his head, exclaiming, "I think it would look great in our bar when it's finished!" As John set it down on the ground, Angela looked at it with disgust. "It's kind of dirty though." John smiled as he proclaimed, "I can clean it off, you know!" Angela reluctantly agreed that they could keep the doll. But not long after bringing the doll in, strange things began to happen within the building. This led to many questions for the couple. Where did the doll come from? More importantly, why was it left behind?

This doll is believed to be inhabited by a spirit. *Author's photo.*

The origin story of this abandoned doll all began with Erwood C. ("Ray") Raysin, who was born on August 10, 1925, to Carl and Amanda (formerly Walterhouse) Raysin in the city of Flint, Michigan. In his late teens, Ray began dating a beautiful young woman named Marion L. Lucas, who was born on August 1, 1926, and was also a Flint native. On September 8, 1945, at ages nineteen and twenty, the two lovebirds wed and moved to Davison together. However, shortly after marrying, Ray, who was enlisted in the U.S. Navy, went on to serve his country during World War II and the Korean War. Despite being away for lengthy periods at a time, the couple went on to have three sons and a daughter together—Tom, Kent, Mike and Teresa. When Ray was not actively serving his country, he worked as a licensed funeral director in Genesee County to provide for his family. By the late 1960s, Ray was one of the most respected funeral directors in all of Michigan, and he and Marion decided that they wanted to open their own funeral home. By 1970, the very first funeral home in Davison was born when the duo founded the Raysin Funeral Home. Ray went on to become a member of the Michigan Funeral Director Association and was invited to join several community organizations, including the Masonic Rite and the Davison Chamber of Commerce. He even served as the president of the Davison Rotary Club. While Ray soothed the everyday depression that came from working with grieving families by engaging in social activities, Marion turned to her love of doll collecting.

Marion first found comfort in dolls during the Great Depression, when she was only five or six years old. After suffering from chronic ear infections as a child, she underwent surgery to remove the mastoid bone behind her left ear. Her financially destitute parents saved up, and after her surgical procedure was finished, they gifted her with her very first doll. Unfortunately, Marion's sisters were enthralled with the doll since they never had one before and ended up breaking it and eventually losing it. As Marion grew older, she began collecting all sorts of dolls, to the point that she was running out of room to store them. Between buying them herself and being gifted them, even by families who held wakes at the Raysin Funeral Home, Marion amassed too many dolls to keep in her home.

In September 1988, one year after the Raysins retired from the funeral business and sold their funeral home to Wayne and Margaret Allen, Marion moved her doll collection to the lower level of 310 North Main Street, as the upper level was being utilized as an apartment, and established a doll museum under the name Auntie M's Collectibles Inc. Hundreds, if not thousands, of dolls sat perched on shelves, sitting on chairs and stacked in piles around the room in their respective boxes. A piano sat among them for Marion to play when she desired to entertain herself and others. The doll museum did not officially open to the public until 2012 and served more as an oasis for Marion and her doll-collecting friends. Throughout Marion's duration as owner of the building, there were times the dolls seemed to take on a life of their own after she would leave for the night. Someone or something would rearrange her dolls and leave them in strange positions, much to her dismay. According to local legend, it is believed that spirits from the old Raysin Funeral Home had attached to some of Marion's dolls.

On the afternoon of Saturday, August 29, 2015, one of Marion's worst nightmares came true when she was informed that her beloved Ray passed away at the age of ninety. At the time, he was under the care of the Jacob's Ladder Assisted Living Community in Grand Blanc. To add salt to her wounds, just a day later, a child living above her doll museum set the apartment ablaze while playing with a lighter and candles. Flames could be seen raging out of the upper windows of the historic structure, according to Davison fire chief Mike Wright, who arrived on scene just minutes after the fire started. The building's interior suffered extensive smoke and water damage. Fortunately, the family got out safely, but the same could not be said for many of Marion's dolls.

A grief-stricken Marion put the surviving dolls in her collection back on display the best that she could with the help of her friends Sally Duquette and Grace Bolin and lived out the rest of her days fine-tuning the museum to her liking. Marion passed away just over a year later on November 14, 2016, also at the age of ninety.

A few days after Marion's passing, a group of repairmen headed down into the basement to do some work, and while down there, they heard the piano playing upstairs. They ran up to see who was in the building but realized that they were all alone and that the piano had actually been playing by itself.

The Hudsons' business, The Agitated Grape, was officially opened on October 23, 2017; the demanding renovations required to open the wine bar had paid off. After spending an agonizing amount of time pulling up various flooring materials and at least three distinct layers of sub-flooring, the Hudsons spent another twenty-six hours pulling up all the nails to reveal the original wooden plank flooring from the 1800s. It was a laborious task but made for a classy-looking establishment for couples and friends to grab a drink and enjoy a night on the town.

Two of the bar's very first customers had a paranormal experience on their first visit. A married couple had come in to enjoy a few glasses of wine and sat down at one of the tables closest to the wall. As they were conversing about their day, one of their wine glasses slid clear across the table and nearly fell to the floor as if someone had a firm hold on it. At first, the customers thought maybe it was due to the gathered condensation beneath the glass, but when the wife caught the glass in midair, she discovered that the chalice and the table were both bone-dry. Another similar experience was had by a server who was tending to a small wedding reception in the back of the building prior to the Hudsons implementing a full kitchen. The server came frantically bolting out to the bar screaming Angela's name in holy terror. "Angela!" "Yes?" Angela asked puzzled. "The cake knife! The wedding party's cake knife! It moved all the way across the table…by itself!" Unsure of what to say or make of the incident, Angela replied with a simple, "Okay." The server desperately expressed that she wasn't joking around. "I promise you; I am not kidding! Everyone saw it move across the table!" "Well, um, that's really weird," Angela answered back, not really knowing what to do. In the twinkling of an eye, Angela began having experiences herself that weren't so easy to explain away.

When the bar first opened, the only food that was served there was on charcuterie boards. These charcuterie boards were made of heavy marble, and on various occasions, one would fall into the metal sink and break. One evening, when Angela was closing up for the night, she heard the distinct echo throughout the building of a heavy marble slab falling into the sink. Upset about the prospect that another one of her boards was broken, she walked over to the sink with a lump in her throat, only to realize that nothing had fallen at all. Everything was still perfectly intact. Then the Hudsons' ADT motion-censored security system began going off on a regular basis in the middle of the night, even when it was verified that no one was causing it

Left: The Irish doll currently watches over the bar at The Agitated Grape. *Author's photo.*

Below: The Agitated Grape's thirty-two-ounce cocktails are worth a visit to the bar. *Angela Hudson of The Agitated Grape.*

Cindy Facknitz standing in front of the door that locks her out and, occasionally, locks her in. *Author's photo.*

to go off. Angela has even occasionally heard heavy doors slamming while in the building by herself, but they were always locked when she'd go investigate. At long last, Angela saw something unusual with her own two eyes. She had been alone in the building and was heading toward the kitchen when she noticed a dark shadow moving through the kitchen's pass-through window. Before long, more employees at the bar began experiencing paranormal phenomena as well.

Angela's sister, Cindy Facknitz, works at the bar part time doing morning food prep and consistently works alone in the building. One of her duties includes going to and from the basement numerous times throughout her shift to get stock. Because of that, she is the only person who carries a key for the basement door. To make the constant running up and down easier on herself, Cindy props the door open so if her hands are full she doesn't have to worry about having to open it, as she can just bump it open with her hip. On countless occasions, Cindy has gone down to the basement and discovered that she has been locked out or, occasionally, locked in. This occurrence seems isolated only to Cindy, as it's never happened to any other staff member—at least not yet.

While in the basement and in the kitchen, Cindy has heard footsteps as if someone is walking across the wooden floors with heavy boots on and has even heard whistling. "It always sounds like it is coming from the center of the building, right on the main floor." One day, while going to investigate the sound, Cindy rounded the corner and saw the bathroom door, which is usually always shut, slowly opening in front of her. "I feel like whatever is going on is pretty innocuous, but I do believe the activity to be essentially residual." The most disconcerting experience Cindy ever had at the bar was the sound of someone entering through the back door, only to discover no one was there at all. "You can distinctly hear the door opening and someone come inside. When that happens, it honestly does creep me out a little. I always feel like I'm being watched."

The mystery of who exactly is inhabiting the Irish doll continues, but it's obviously someone who has a strong affinity for the building itself and refuses to leave. The paranormal happenings are strongly linked to the doll's presence. To this day, the porcelain toy sits high above the bar, keeping a close eye on all who enter. Make sure to say hello to the spirit that dwells deep within on your next jaunt to The Agitated Grape, and while you're at it, make sure to try one of the bar's famous giant cocktails, including a massive mimosa and bloody Mary—consisting of thirty-two ounces of pure Michigan liquor stacked high with everything from pizza to doughnuts to vegetables. After all, who doesn't enjoy a little spirit when it comes to their booze?

TEQUILA WITH A SIDE OF TERROR

FIESTA MEXICANA RESTAURANT & CANTINA

1820 LANSING ROAD
CHARLOTTE, MI 48813

J ust a little over twenty miles from Michigan's metropolis, Lansing, sits the city of Charlotte. With a population of just over nine thousand, Charlotte is your "average Jane" of cities, with blue-collar workers, comfortable homes and apartments, hair salons, grocery stores and great schools. Not too far within the city, on Lansing Road, sits a Mexican-themed restaurant called Fiesta Mexicana Restaurant & Cantina. This establishment is most associated with being the Alpine Bar, which was founded in the mid-1940s, but it's had many different names over the years, including Rockinghams, Dawgg Haus, Cactus Juice Steakhouse, Hot Shots, Big Time Bar and The Stockyard BBQ and Brew. It even briefly served as an antique mall before becoming the Mexican restaurant and cantina we know it as today. Despite the various names and themes over the years, the property has been plagued with intense amounts of paranormal activity.

On Sunday, February 12, 1989, Nora Rashid, the beloved owner of the Alpine Bar, passed away in a nearby hospital after battling a terminal illness for half a decade. She was eighty-seven years old, and her frail body could not fight any longer. When the current owner, Terry Ranshaw, purchased the property in 1994, he was incorrectly informed by a local that Mrs. Rashid had passed away in the building. It wasn't that anyone was intentionally trying to lie to Terry. In fact, the individual who told him that had honestly

Nora Rashid's headstone. *Katie Benghauser.*

believed it, and that's because he saw her ghost on every visit to the property after her death.

The first employee Terry hired to work for him was a young woman from the surrounding neighborhood. On her first day, Terry was working on something in the dining room while the new hire filled out some paperwork in one of the two offices in the back of the building that are adjacent to the kitchen. When the employee looked up from the desk, a bespectacled elderly lady with black bouffant hair was standing in front of her. Assuming it was another worker Terry had hired, the young woman greeted the elderly woman with a friendly "Hello!" in an attempt to make a good first impression. The older lady smiled warmly, said hello in return and then proceeded to walk straight through the wall and disappear.

Terry's employee began screaming at the top of her lungs and emerged from the kitchen doors with the color completely drained from her face. "What's going on?!" he asked, alarmed, taken off guard by the commotion. The young employee wailed in hysteria as she motioned to the area behind herself with trembling hands: "That lady back there just walked through the damn wall!" Grabbing the back of a chair to steady herself, she took a deep breath, still in disbelief at what she had just witnessed. Terry tried to rationalize the peculiar happening, as he hadn't had his own paranormal experience at this point, but it was no use. After fifteen minutes of sitting with his employee and attempting to calm her down to no avail, she stood up and announced that the job was not a good fit for her and promptly took off out the door.

By 2014, the establishment was at its peak of paranormal activity, and almost all ten of Ranshaw's employees had encountered something paranormal. Heather McCumber, who worked as the kitchen manager, began to see Mrs. Rashid so often that she nicknamed her "Rosie." She didn't know anything about Nora Rashid, but all her experiences with the ghost were benevolent. According to Heather, "Rosie" had a habit of turning the lights on and off at all hours of the day and night. However, when staff began dropping off the schedule like flies and waiter Jessica Bailey began refusing to close down the restaurant by herself, Terry suspected that something darker was at play.

He made several frantic calls to the Tri-City Ghost Hunters Society (TCGHS) in June 2014, always leaving a voicemail after each call during which he detailed the insane amounts of activity his staff had experienced over his duration as the building's owner and pleaded for the team to come out and do a paranormal investigation. His employees were encountering such frightening phenomena that when TCGHS asked if they would like to join in on an investigation, they adamantly refused. The reports included mirrors flying off the wall, appliances being used without anyone in sight, broken dishes scattered across the kitchen, messes appearing out of nowhere and poltergeist-like activity with furniture moving and loud machinery being triggered when people were alone in the building. The most feared experience, and most popular, was the sighting of a malicious, shapeshifting shadow figure.

Members of TCGHS were certainly interested in the opportunity and thankful that Terry believed in their abilities to help him, but they weren't initially expecting anything to happen. They had come off a string of cases prior to this one where people cried wolf and they didn't even get a puppy. The team would always go into investigations with an open mind and try to maintain a sense of neutrality. After going into several locations across the United States, some even known as the "most haunted" locations in the country, and spending countless hours and days in them with not even a single experience to write home about, they began to feel discouraged. Nonetheless, TCGHS had a job to do.

The team packed their equipment bags and made their way from Bay City, Michigan, to what was then The Stockyard BBQ and Brew, a popular southwestern-themed hangout for young and old "cowboys and cowgirls at heart" with live country music performers and a bar full of seemingly endless liquors. Upon arriving, they got a tour of the entire building. When you walked through the front doors, you were greeted by the main dining hall. To the right was a warm and inviting fireplace that drew you in and led you to the opposite corner, where there was a makeshift stage. Along the left wall stretched the bar, with stools lined up for guests to sit. If you continued walking around the right-hand corner of the bar, you would have come to a pathway with doors at the end that led to the kitchen and the conjoined back offices. Once the tour was finished, the staff, one by one, left for the night. Harold Beauchamp, the team's tech manager, set up the equipment to perfection and shut off the lights.

The rest of what I'm about to tell you will be almost too hard to believe; however, it is all true. To date, it's one of the most jaw-dropping paranormal investigations the team ever took part in.

The crew were locked in by management, and the restaurant was in a secluded part of the city, so there wasn't a lot of interference from traffic and bystanders. They started the investigation in the dining portion of the building, having cameras aimed at the bar and pathway to the kitchen, as well as toward the front of the building at the fireplace across from the stage.

The fireplace was said to be one of the hot spots of paranormal activity according to Terry and his staff. It was a few hours into the investigation, and in the semi-darkness, the team began noticing activity. As the members of TCGHS sat beckoning the spirits to come forth, the décor of cowboy hats on the wall above the bar seemed to move, making everyone uneasy. During this time, investigator Ellen Beauchamp could also see a short shadow figure pacing back and forth behind the bar. It ducked down every now and then, as if it was playing a game of hide-and-seek. The air felt stale as she watched the movement with wide eyes.

During the time the activity was picking up, the team was recording audio from two different ends of the same room. Occasionally, this is done to document discrepancies between any evidence captured. Harold decided to get up and change out the batteries of one of the motion sensor cameras that was sitting on the bar. It was also a good opportunity for him to confront the shadow figure that seemed so amused at keeping Ellen on edge. Harold crept up to the bar and stood still, so as not to disturb any activity they were

A lot of paranormal activity transpires around this bar. *David Ranshaw of Fiesta Mexicana Restaurant & Cantina (formerly The Stockyard BBQ and Brew).*

already getting. Everyone sat still, hardly daring to breathe as the barstool lifted off the ground and hovered about a foot and a half in the air for a split second before crashing to the ground aggressively. In a trice, the ear-splitting sound of a ligneous barstool clashing to the floor pierced everyone's ears. Harold was in a state of shock, as this occurred only inches away from him. He briefly shone his flashlight on the barstool and discovered that the seat of the chair was about three feet from its original location and that the back of it was facing the complete opposite direction, as if something with superhuman strength had picked it up from the backrest and slammed it down in a fit of rage. A few moments later, a short shadow figure was spotted scampering along the backlit wall on the pathway to the kitchen. The most peculiar thing about this figure was that it moved in a fashion that defied logic. It was as if it floated to the back of the establishment at record speed. It never took a single step.

Later that evening, the team investigated the back offices and were sitting in a circle conducting an EVP (electronic voice phenomena) session when it sounded like someone slammed the inside of the window with their two hands. Upon closer inspection, the frosted outline of two handprints was imprinted on the inside of the glass, facing the investigators. They immediately stopped the session and got up to explore the premises. They could not find anyone. They even went out of the emergency exit to cover all their bases, but lo and behold, the city sat desolate and silent in the night. The team was completely alone—and yet they were not.

A short while later, it sounded like a full-blown dinner party was happening just through the doors leading to the restaurant. The team sat with darting eyes, unable to speak as they listened to what sounded like women gossiping with one another, men laughing over their cigars and toasts being made in a celebration. In addition to their soft, haunting voices, when they closed their eyes, they could almost hear the noises of the Wild West—the sounds of plates and cutlery clinking and heels walking elegantly across the floor filled the air. It was all so very loud! It sounded as if the bar was open for business and the TCGHS crew were the only ones who didn't get the memo. After a few seconds of listening to the chaos happening in the restaurant, the team had to know what was going on out there. Surely people must have snuck in!

Upon rushing out of the office, through the kitchen doors and into the restaurant, with flashlights clutched in their hands, they discovered that there wasn't a crowd, nor were there any other people in the building besides them. The restaurant doors were still tightly locked, and the silence was so thick you could have cut it with a knife.

It was as if the investigators were being watched by an army of people they couldn't even see. Ellen grabbed both recorders that had been left running on both ends of the restaurant and played them back in the hopes that she had captured the lively dinner party that had happened just moments before.

Not only was the audio of the dinner party captured, but both recorders also revealed different audio during the same timestamp, despite being left in the same room! The recorder left closest to the bar lacked any disembodied voices, and the other, left by the fireplace, contained two menacing-sounding males that mocked Ellen when she asked if the spirits knew Terry's name. When Ellen mentioned that Terry was the owner of the building, one of the entities also snickered and muttered sarcastically, "Sure he is."

Both voices were gravelly and wicked, leaving the team's souls almost feeling blackened and tarnished by something they could not fight back even if they wanted. Terry believed there to be only one resident spirit—the ghost of Nora Rashid—but the TCGHS team captured something much darker on their recorders. The distant voices that had been recorded were enough to chill anyone's blood.

In the Greater Lansing area alone, there are some impressive locations that are rumored to be haunted. Nearly the whole of Michigan State University's campus has been swirling with legends of paranormal activity for decades. In the oldest residence hall that's still in use on the campus, called Mary Mayo Hall, there are reports of a piano playing by itself, and a female apparition is frequently witnessed in the West lounge. There was a student who lost his life during World War II who is believed to be the one to ring the bells in Beaumont Tower in search of the lover he left behind.

Michigan's state capitol is purportedly haunted by Tommaso Juglaris, an Italian artist who painted the rotunda. The sighting of his ghost is accompanied by cold, stagnant air.

The Bath Consolidated School witnessed a massacre at the hands of Andrew P. Kehoe on May 18, 1927, after he spent months placing dynamite and pyrotol beneath the school's flooring. Kehoe also suicide-bombed himself on the school's property during this act of evil by shooting a rifle into the backseat of his truck, which had also been loaded with dynamite. Thirty-eight elementary school children and six adults, including Kehoe, were brutally murdered in what was the most heinous mass murder to take place in a school in the history of the United States. Spectral children have been spotted playing on the property, taking pleasure in the joys of a life that was taken away from them far too soon.

Considering all these incredibly haunted places in the same region of Michigan and the captivating ghost lore that follows them, you may wonder what made The Stockyard BBQ and Brew any different. For starters, it has not yet been a stop on a ghost tour. Its ghost stories had been mentioned in a local paper or two, but it has never been plastered nationally all over the major media outlets as being insanely haunted. Lastly, paranormal reality television stars were not flooding through the doors in droves with the hopes of one-upping one another on the best caught evidence. It was a place that, until now, has been rather obscure, and yet the frequency of apparition sightings is greater than all three of the previously mentioned locations combined.

Many in the Greater Lansing area have speculated that the multiple entities present at the bar, along with the sinister shadow figure, had been customers of the Alpine Bar back when it was in operation. It was rumored that there was one man who deeply suffered from alcoholism who would always get kicked out of the bar for initiating fights with other patrons. Many believe that he still lingers around because he is eagerly waiting to exact revenge on Mrs. Rashid.

Terry's son, David, who saw the entity of who he presumes is the raging alcoholic, described him as a black shadow figure wearing a long coat and cowboy hat.

In February 2015, the back portion of the building experienced a mysterious fire that not even the fire marshals could figure out. Unfortunately, the fire resulted in the demise of the business known as The Stockyard BBQ and Brew. After an investment of a lot of time and money, the back portion of the building was able to be rebuilt. The continuous renovations and improvements have also kept the paranormal activity alive and well. The sightings of the sweet Mrs. Rashid and the menacing shadow figure persist, as do the reports of hearing spectral conversations. If you're lucky enough to visit the great state of Michigan and drop by the cantina, you'll have your chance to dine with the dead. Hopefully the soul present at your table will be Mrs. Rashid and not the entity that plays harmless jokes by day and terrorizes people at night. Make sure to exercise good table manners, as you never know who is watching you.

TWO MARTINIS WITH A SHOT OF MISOGYNY

MARLEY'S BAR & GRILL

127 WALNUT STREET
MANISTIQUE, MI 49854

O ne of Manistique's oldest taverns, currently named Marley's Bar & Grill, surprisingly, has not witnessed many human tragedies. Yet it is still riddled with paranormal activity. It was built in the early 1890s, prior to the great fire of September 15, 1893, that ravaged the streets of Manistique. Not long before midnight, someone with clearly nothing better to do and a hell of a lot of flammable liquid made their way down Walnut Street and snuck behind Paul Rediker's Saloon. In a moment of utter madness, they decided that they were going to burn Manistique to the ground. Dousing the side of the building with copious amounts of this liquid, believed to be either gasoline or coal oil, the individual lit a match and threw it against the building. The flames lit up the night sky as the arsonist crept off quietly into the night. This resulted in twenty-two businesses being demolished and five families winding up homeless. The building that would later become Marley's was one of them. Thankfully, there were no casualties, and the village was eventually rebuilt. With that all being said, if no one died in this monstrous fire, how could the bar possibly be so haunted? What is really causing this unusual phenomenon? The short answer is: women.

Before the great fire nearly annihilated the village, the Ed Nessman Saloon was the original saloon to occupy what was then 200 Walnut Street. The word *Svensk* was proudly painted above the door advertising that Swedish

Above: The Ed Nessman Saloon on Walnut Street, circa the late 1800s. *Schoolcraft County Historical Society.*

Opposite: The original safe bearing the J.B. Held namesake remains in the bar to this day. *Mary Lou Hoffman of Marley's Bar & Grill.*

was spoken there. In 1892, at the age of sixteen, Henry T. Jahn immigrated to the land of Uncle Sam from Sonnenberg, Germany, with the goal of moving to Manistique. Once settled in, he became business partners with J.B. Held, and together they operated a tavern. It didn't take long for Henry to learn the ropes of the industry because he became the proprietor of his own establishment, Jahn's Bar. After coming into ownership, he made a home on the second level of the building.

The legal drinking age was not regulated in Michigan until the early part of the twentieth century, and even the few states that did implement a minimum drinking age at the time rarely enforced those laws. So, while it seems odd to most people that Jahn was operating bars as a teenager, it wasn't inappropriate during that era.

It has been widely rumored that Jahn's Bar started out with very little to offer in terms of comfort. Apparently, there was nowhere to sit, no way to call out in the event of an emergency and no jukebox to play tunes. So long as you were able-bodied enough to stand, the bar would be happy to serve

you—if you could not, well, you'd have to take your business elsewhere. The bar was also certainly not a place you could go and try to meet a companion. It wasn't commonplace during that era for women to hang out in bars, and Henry held deeply misogynistic views that women had their places—any female worth respecting most definitely wouldn't be caught dead in one, he thought. If he ever saw a woman trying to come in, he would fiercely demand that she get lost and chase her away. He also felt that these wayward women would not make suitable wives and deemed them "rabble-rousers." But the drinks were strong and kept the hardworking men in Manistique coming back time and time again.

The bar reportedly also provided bank services to locals. Individuals could enjoy a hearty glass of whiskey and cash their checks all in one go. The original safe purportedly used to cash the checks still sits in the establishment today bearing the name of Henry's business partner.

In 1898, Henry fought in the Spanish-American War and was also a commander of the Spanish War Veterans Post. He also was involved with the Soldiers' and Sailors' Relief Commission for a multitude of years. All the while, he kept his bar up and running successfully.

On November 20, 1900, Henry married Frances Weber, and together they had five children. Their son Norman, often called "Normie," was born in 1907 and took an interest in his father's business from an early age. After graduating in 1926 from Manistique High School, he experimented with different careers in different cities around the state before deciding to become business partners with his father. The bar's name was then changed to Henry Jahn and Son. Norman was taught that under no exceptions was a woman allowed into the bar, and he became a stickler himself for enforcing that very rule.

Between Henry getting older and Norman starting a family of his own, the partnership worked well, as each man could depend on the other to step up and help when things got rough. This especially proved to be true when Norman's three-year-old son, David, passed away at the Children's Clinic in Marquette after suffering from a three-week-long illness. He was rushed to the hospital in critical condition and given a blood transfusion, but his condition worsened and he ended up passing away on January 31, 1941. As Norman took time to mourn the loss of his child, he knew that his dad would keep the business going strong. The two men made a great team and worked together up until Henry wound up hospitalized. He had not been feeling well for months and was admitted to the Veterans Administration Hospital in Iron Mountain only two days prior to his death on Friday, July 18, 1958.

The business name was once again changed back to Jahn's Bar and later was referred to as Jahn's Saloon. Norman lived out the rest of his days dabbling in politics (he sat on the county board of commissioners as a city supervisor) and operating a male-only establishment up until he died on

Behind the bar closest to the right is Normie. His father, Henry, stands directly to his left wearing a shirt and tie. The men were hosting a St. Patrick's Day celebration at the bar during the late 1940s. *Mary Lou Hoffman of Marley's Bar & Grill.*

June 27, 1989. It was during this time that his eldest son, Norman B. Jahn Jr., a high school teacher, took over ownership of the bar and called it Norm's. Then, just a few years after his father's death, in 1992, Norman Jr. passed away as well.

After Norman Jr.'s death, the bar changed hands a few different times and was given various names. With each name change also came a more progressive change of rules.

In 2001, Mary Lou Hoffman, who had worked as an automotive engineer for twenty years, found out that she was being laid off from her job. Rather than despair, she thought it over and decided that it was time for a career change. Instead of waiting for retirement to relocate to the picturesque shores of Manistique, she expedited the process by purchasing Marley's Bar in June of that same year. Mary decided to keep the name of the bar, as it reminded her of Jacob Marley from *A Christmas Carol*, and decided to deck out the bar with a Victorian Christmas theme that could be enjoyed all year long.

This bar was not only her new workplace but also somewhere she could call home. Now that a strong and determined woman was calling the shots around the bar, it riled up the spirit of Norman Jahn Sr.

Mary Lou's first paranormal incident happened when the bar was open to the public, but she and her employee were the only ones on site. There weren't a lot of people out and about, so Mary Lou thought that she would have no issue quickly popping over to the bar next door. When she returned, the back door was locked. Thankful that she had her keys on her, she inserted the key into the doorknob and unlocked the door, but then she realized that the door had been deadbolted. As she went to unlock the deadbolt, she could hear the doorknob lock again. She proceeded once again to unlock the doorknob when she heard the deadbolt latch. Thinking it was her employee messing with her, she began shouting at him through the door, but when she opened the door mere seconds later, her employee stood what felt like more than one hundred feet away from her at the bar. "He saw my face and knew something was amiss, and the ghost had got me. He couldn't have run that fast to get from the door to the bar, especially going around a corner."

Mary Lou had another encounter with the spirit one Thanksgiving. It was broad daylight, and Mary Lou and her friends had been waiting for a few additional pals to arrive at the bar. While everyone sat around the table mingling, they could hear someone pounding on the back door. Everyone looked at one another confused, as the door wasn't locked and whoever it was could have easily just walked in. A decent amount of time had passed and no one entered the bar, but the pounding started up again. *Ugh! I guess I'll go let them in!*, Mary Lou thought to herself as she stood up from her chair annoyed. When she got to the back door and swung it open, no one was there. No one could be seen in either the parking lot or alleyway either. Eventually, her pals did show up and came to the front door.

In the fifteen years that Mary Lou lived on the second floor above the bar, she never had anything paranormal happen up there. She believes that her paranormal encounters are isolated to the main floor. A former employee has a different story.

In the early spring of 2021, Mary Lou hired a woman to work as the bar manager, and they had an agreement that the woman would work at Marley's for a minimum of six months. Another part of the agreement was that she would be moving into the apartment upstairs. The woman arrived by mid-May and was excited to begin working. As the days went on, Mary Lou couldn't help but notice that she was visibly unhappy. It wasn't long before she worked out that her employee was not getting any sleep.

Evening after evening, the woman would undergo a series of terrorizing events—from a heavy salt lamp that was repeatedly tossed around by unseen hands to obnoxiously loud noises of someone rampaging through the housing unit that would keep her awake for the whole night. Sleeping there became impossible. The manager could not specify what room in the apartment these noises were coming from, but they were getting harder and harder to ignore. After just a few weeks of enduring the nuisance in the apartment, she dropped the bomb on Mary Lou that she was resigning. She planned to stay in the apartment for a week longer, only to give her enough time to gather up her things and find new housing arrangements. On her last night in the apartment, as she lay awake in the darkness listening to a ruckus being made in the next room over, she decided that she had dealt with enough. She packed an overnight bag and headed toward the staircase. Just before making it down the stairs, she was overcome by a feeling of discontentment when a partition wall that had been standing solid for the entire duration of her stay came crashing down at her. It felt deliberate. Shuddering from head to toe, she took off running down the stairs, flung the outside door open and never looked back. She left just prior to Fathers' Day on Sunday, June 20.

Mary generally chalks the spooky happenings at the establishment up to Norman either having a puckish sense of humor or being unhappy. In this

Liquor bottles and glasses tend to fly around at Marley's. *Mary Lou Hoffman of Marley's Bar & Grill.*

specific situation, she believes it was the latter. "Normie mustn't have liked her for some reason."

Other employees have witnessed empty barstools spinning at full pelt, bottles and glasses being cast into shards and important cooking tools disappearing from the kitchen at wildly inconvenient intervals. Many customers have reported feeling a masculine, iron-fisted presence while in the bar, with one guy claiming that he could physically feel someone standing behind him. Another customer was told off with obscenities by a disembodied voice after bad-mouthing one of the workers. While the ghost of Norman Jahn Sr. evidently enjoys giving everyone who enters a run for their money, Mary Lou doesn't find him to be all that malevolent, at least not with her. "Normie must feel he needs to protect the bar or maybe just wants things a certain way."

For the thrill-seeking ladies who desire a more elevated spine-tingling experience, Mary Lou has converted the second floor into an Airbnb that can be rented out. So come out for a few drinks and see if you can withstand the night at Marley's Bar & Grill. After all, it is the twenty-first century—someone needs to tell Norman that a woman's place is wherever she wants it to be.

East Coast Scare

The Side Door Saloon at The Blue Pelican Inn & Restaurant

2535 North Main Street
Central Lake, MI 49622

About thirty-nine miles north of Traverse City, in Antrim County, sits the village of Central Lake. It's a scenic and secluded little place away from the hustle and bustle of the big cities. One of the village's most popular and historic lodging destinations, The Blue Pelican Inn, provides shelter for those road-tripping in the summer or passing through in the winter. With creative events, mouthwatering food and a variety of drinks, it's no wonder the inn is a favorite among travelers. But it seems the busier it gets, the more the inn comes to life with its many supernatural tenants, and those who've dined and stayed the night there have gotten way more than they bargained for.

On June 14, 1922, L. Van Skiver, a fishing enthusiast from the village of Ellsworth, posted an advertisement in the *Detroit Free Press* offering five dollars to anyone who could come up with the best name for a fishing resort. He desired to create a comfortable and serene retreat that would be surrounded by lakes. Not long after the advertisement was published, Van Skiver's plan came to fruition when his new resort was erected in Central Lake. The resort was initially named the We-Go-Ta-Hotel and later the Central Lake Hotel, and it was listed in the newspaper as having twenty rooms for guests with a dining room that held a capacity of one hundred people. Since Van Skiver spent so much time in Central Lake, it was inevitable that he would end up befriending the locals. While out networking, he met the owner of the Central Lake Canning Factory, Emmons Butler ("E.B.") Gill.

As the friendship progressed, Mr. Gill and his wife, Helen Mary ("Nellie"), took up residence in the new structure and began assisting with operations. For several years, the hotel doubled as a boardinghouse, and many people passed through its doors. In good times and bad times, the backbone of the hotel came together for the greater good of the community.

When Central Lake High School went up in flames in February 1927, there was a $75,000 loss in property damage, records

Emmons Butler ("E.B.") Gill. *Chris Corbett of The Blue Pelican Inn.*

and materials. The educational faculty were extremely hard-pressed to find an empty building to set up a makeshift school considering there was record attendance that year. Unfortunately, they were unable to find a vacant building to use but were presented with the opportunity to use the hotel as a temporary school, as it was quite spacious. In the 1920s, it is estimated that about 75 percent of adolescents, even children as young as ten years old, went to high schools to be educated, so having an adequate space to accommodate all the students was crucial. Once a new school had been rebuilt and the students had left, this act of generosity inspired Van Skiver to explore other amenities that the hotel could offer to the public.

The first tavern was implemented on the property in 1930 and was advertised in local newspapers three years before Prohibition officially ended. Van Skiver decided that he would head the tavern as manager, and the Gills would become more heavily involved with the day-to-day operations. After all, they were totally in love with the building and were excited about the new addition, believing it would provide steady revenue for the hotel.

Soon, crowds of weary travelers and locals looking to quench their thirst were coming to the resort. And each time they would visit, a familiar face would greet them as they ascended the steps of the front porch. A young girl, about elementary school age, with sparkling eyes and rosy cheeks, habitually stood in the double hung dormer windows of the attic, clutching her schoolbooks to her chest as she looked out at the incoming guests, her plump pink lips upturned in a smile. She excitedly watched with eyes as big as saucers as some of them hauled suitcases full of treasures, as now she would have someone and something to play with. What the incoming guests did not know when they smiled back at her was that she was dead.

Many speculate if the child was an undocumented victim of the fire or simply a young girl who enjoyed learning and died far too young from other causes. No one really knows for sure, but whatever the cause of death, her presence in the attic windows became the very first reported paranormal sighting at the hotel. It didn't take long before the spirits began multiplying.

On February 23, 1942, at the age of seventy-eight, Mr. Gill passed away. Heartsick, Mrs. Gill left the hotel for a few years to clear her mind, before feeling a compulsion to return. She must have known that her heart was going to fail because on March 16, 1951, Mrs. Gill died at eighty-four years old in the basement of the place she loved the most: the Central Lake Hotel.

The hotel switched hands various times throughout the years, undergoing many renovations, floor plan modifications and name changes, with the last being Murphy's Lamplight Inn. When the Murphys vacated the building, fate would have it that it fell into the lap of the current owner, Chris Corbett, and his wife, Merrie.

When Albion native Merrie first convinced her Virginian husband to take annual trips to Central Lake in the mid-1970s, he never realized how much he would fall in love with the place. Before they knew it, the couple had become business owners in the area. One of those businesses was The Blue Pelican Restaurant, which was opened in 2003 and was lovingly named after Chris's favorite restaurant back in Virginia, Black Pelican Seafood Company. The Corbetts were elated to bring the delectable cuisine of the East Coast to an area of Michigan that they loved so much. The villagers of Central Lake seemed to really enjoy it too. However, much to the dismay of the Corbetts, their well-liked establishment was swallowed by flames on July 29, 2008, when red squirrels invaded the attic and ate up the Romex wiring. Chris Corbett didn't have time to sulk about his losses after, as he was approached by prominent townspeople, including the mayor, who were encouraging him to purchase the historic hotel. Because the hotel was going into foreclosure, Chris was presented with an inexpensive offer that he could not refuse. And with that offer, the Corbetts were thrust into a paranormal hurricane when they purchased the property, now known as The Blue Pelican Inn, in October of that same year.

"I'm Catholic and I heard plenty of talk around the town that the building was haunted, but I did not believe in it until I had my first experience," Chris said, inhaling sharply as he sat deep in thought for a moment. As

MRS. E. B. GILL DIES— Funeral services were held Monday at the Diton funeral home at Central Lake for Mrs Helen Gill, 84, mother of Miss Allena E. Gill of Detroit and Mrs. G. W. Harsch of Saginaw, formerly of this city, whose death occurred at the Central Lake hotel which she formerly operated. Burial was made there in Southern cemetery. Mrs Gill had been a resident of Central Lake for about 50 years, and was long prominent in Congregational church activities and Order of Eastern Star circles. Surviving, besides the two daughters are a son, Gordon Elwood Gill of Grand Rapids; seven grandchildren; two great grandchildren and a sister, Mrs. Mary Story of Olean, N. Y. Mr. Gill, who was owner and manager of the Central Lake Canning factory died February 23, 1912.

Left: Mrs. E.B. Gill's death announcement confirming her passing at the Central Lake Hotel. *Paul Heidbreder of the* Traverse City Record-Eagle.

Right: Helen Mary ("Nellie") Gill. *Chris Corbett of The Blue Pelican Inn.*

he slowly exhaled, he continued, "Neighboring businesses always asked me who the child was standing in the window, and I didn't know what they were talking about at first. My first paranormal encounter happened when we were doing construction to remodel the inn. That was the first day I believe I encountered the little girl."

Chris was seeking a place to hang his "Blue Pelican" neon sign that was salvaged from the fire at his restaurant. After thinking about it, he thought that the dormer windows would be the perfect place, so he planned to remove the windows and replace the open area with siding on which he could hang the sign. When the day came, a carpenter friend came to help. After dislodging the windows, both men counted to three preparing to throw each window into the dump truck below. When they got to the count of three, Chris felt one of his shoulders dislocate. He recovered just fine but thought that the timing of it was odd, especially considering he had exerted far more physical energy and strength during other tasks with no injuries whatsoever. "I could seriously feel my shoulder rip away from its socket. At that moment, I felt like she was punishing me for getting rid of those windows." After the window

The Blue Pelican in recent years. *Chris Corbett of The Blue Pelican Inn.*

incident, Chris could feel a strong electrical current run through his body when passing through certain areas of the building, and there were times his dog, Heart, obsessively watched doors of rooms that Chris was in until the pooch passed out from exhaustion.

A few weeks after the anterior attic windows were covered, the bartender stepped outside the rear entrance of the building to have a cigarette. As his eyes wandered across the building, he noticed movement on the second floor in the second window from the left. As he looked closer, he could make out that a child was staring back at him. The other employees went to check it out and realized that not only was a shade covering the window, but a wall was also built in front of it along with a shower. In addition to appearing in the upstairs windows, the little girl likes to sing, and her airy vocals can be heard echoing down the inn's hallways or singing along to songs she recognizes on the radio. But she mustn't be too loud because Mrs. Gill is always listening.

It was apparent there was more than one spirit on the premises when two employees who were sitting at an upstairs desk heard the printer power on and watched a paper be fed through, only to reveal a single typed "hello."

Although Mrs. Gill roams all floors of the inn, her ghost is most notably seen and heard within The Side Door Saloon and its designated restroom, which is approximately where she took her last breath. Of course, the floor plan has changed a bit since Mrs. Gill's tenancy, but she appears to have

The Side Door Saloon. *Chris Corbett of The Blue Pelican Inn.*

adapted well. People catch her taking care of business out of the corner of their eyes, but when they glance up, she's gone. And while she is not out to intimidate anyone, female bar goers have long advised one another to use the toilet before coming to The Blue Pelican Inn because of awkward happenings in the three-stall restroom.

On regular occasions, women have gone to the bathroom by themselves only to realize that they were not alone. While using an end stall, they would hear the voice of an elderly lady in the middle stall. From sighs to groans to whispering, it's obvious that someone else was in there with them, but each time an intrepid woman would look for legs beneath the stall, her eyes would be met with nothing more than the base of the toilet. One customer even ran out of the bathroom screaming because she heard what sounded like someone sighing noisily into her ear while she was answering nature's call.

Another customer believes that they caught photographic evidence of Mrs. Gill on their camera. While taking photos down at the bar, the customer captured a shot of people standing in line waiting for a drink; beside one woman appears to be a spirit in an old-fashioned cream-colored frock. The spirit was noticeably hovering in the air with no distinguishable legs to hold her up.

It's also believed that Mrs. Gill can be a bit destructive when she doesn't like what's happening around the inn. One night, the cooks left in a hurry, forgetting to put some butter away that was sitting on the countertop. When the chef returned in the morning and saw the butter lying on the floor, he wanted to find out which employee left it like that. After reviewing the security cameras, he could see the butter get swiped off the counter at about 2:30 in the morning, but not a person was in sight. Long story short: don't mess with Mrs. Gill's dairy!

The last two spirits seen around the inn are that of a mysterious man in a tuxedo and a bloodied young girl wearing a fancy dress. The man has been known to appear to certain people, but not everyone. One employee held a door open for him but was given odd looks since she was the only one who could see him and no one else understood what she was doing. He was also seen in the bar enjoying a glass of booze only to vanish moments later. The young lady in a fancy dress has been spotted outside by the entrance and sometimes even crawling down the rooftop of the second story. Rumor has it that she stayed at the inn back when it was a boardinghouse. She was planning to elope with her boyfriend, and as she was climbing down a ladder from the second story, she slipped on the hem of her dress and fell to her death. Her wounded appearance occasionally startles unsuspecting guests, especially those who've had a few too many cocktails.

The reason for all these sightings? Many blame it on the "ghost closet." The closet holds relics of the building's history and has earned its nickname by Blue Pelican staff. For years, psychics and paranormal investigators have believed it to be a portal to the other side, allowing apparitions of the inn's past to come back and visit anytime they wish. Full-bodied apparitions have been traversing through the closet at all hours of the night. While it's no doubt the Corbetts have brought an East Coast flair to Michigan's Northwest region, it appears that they brought the scare along with it.

Spirits, Skulls and Cider

The C-Pub and Fourth Coast Ciderworks at Canterbury Village

The C-Pub
2325 Joslyn Court
Lake Orion, MI 48360

Fourth Coast Ciderworks
2365 Joslyn Court
Lake Orion, MI 48360

Everyone has a "happy place." For many Michiganders, their happy place is a designated historical landmark in Orion Township known as Canterbury Village. The delectable scent of warm cinnamon sugar fills the air from the Yates Cider Mill. Couples say "I do" in fairytale weddings at the Kings Court Castle. Children's eyes light up at the swirling of the carousel as they stuff their mouths with fluffy cotton candy. And friends get together to shop 'til they drop at the many boutiques on the property, ending their exciting day with a beer at the C-Pub or a hard cider at Fourth Coast Ciderworks. But beneath the façade of the many smiling faces lie the deep, dark secrets of the property itself. Since the land was settled, many individuals have reported myriad paranormal happenings. Every building on site has a story; honestly, if the walls of these buildings could talk, I don't know that we would want to listen. Let's just say that the origins of Canterbury Village were the furthest thing from a "happy place."

It was around the year 1840 when Englishman Isaac Haddrill; his wife, Elizabeth; and several of their young children first arrived in the United States. They had made a grueling and tumultuous transatlantic journey during which they survived a shipwreck. In spite of their many hardships, the Haddrills sought a better life and strongly believed that America was the place that they would find it. Since Mr. Haddrill had previously worked as a drover and worked on farms for most of his life, he gravitated toward Southeast Michigan, which was believed to have some of the best farmland in the entire state. He initially purchased forty acres of land and was looking forward to creating a newfound life with his family. From that day forward, Haddrill began preparing the land to build his ideal farm. He built a log cabin for his family to reside in until his wealth increased. Unbeknownst to him, the land was surrounded by Native Americans, and Haddrill most definitely was not a fan.

Haddrill harbored extremely racist feelings toward the natives and became frustrated by their presence near his home. One day, while he was walking around the property, he came across a sharp point sticking up near his feet. "What is this?" he said as he crouched down to inspect the mystery object. After clearing away some soil, he yanked a single flint arrow up from the damp earth. As he held the jagged ammunition in his hand, he looked at it with disgust, knowing that the natives had traversed his recently purchased land. Wanting to rid the land of these objects, Haddrill began plowing through the land to see what else he could uncover. Haddrill discovered not only more Native American relics but also a sacred burial ground just a stone's throw away from his cabin. After coming across numerous human skulls, Haddrill became incandescent with rage, odiously kicking the skulls out of his sight. Dead or alive, the Native Americans were not welcome to be anywhere on his farm. Despite his efforts to be thorough and remove all the bodies off the property, it is believed that many were missed; some even speculate that there may be more than one burial ground within present-day Canterbury Village.

Over the years, the Haddrills expanded their family along with their farm. By 1870, the original Haddrill farmhouse had been established. The original log cabin was torn down and rebuilt as a farmhouse, with the original windows and doors utilized in the construction. It would go on to be painted sky blue and house Revival Salon. The building currently housing the C-Pub, which is also known as the Clansman Gaelic Pub, is believed to be one of the oldest buildings on the property, according to local historians, and was used as a barn. For many years, the two buildings have been inundated with spirits.

The mound of land pictured in this 2022 photograph of Canterbury Village purportedly contains the remains of Native Americans. *Author's photo.*

According to legend, shadow figures would be seen traveling from the farmhouse to the barn, and members of the Haddrill family were sporadically encircled by a cloud of black fog that seemed to appear out of nowhere. The family began taking turns tending to chores in the barn, but while they were in the building alone, they would hear the faint sound of a woman sobbing. Because farming injuries were common, they thought it likely was coming from outside. Each time they would go and check on their other family members, everyone appeared to be okay. On an especially gloomy day, there was a situation in which one of the grown Haddrill children went out to feed the animals, and about five minutes later, they heard an interminable wailing that was louder than anything they had ever heard before. Searching for the source of the sound in the caliginous structure, their eyes fixated on the sight of a woman with long wavy black hair who was kneeling with her head resting in her hands. "State your reason for being here, trespasser!" the Haddrill child demanded coldly. As the woman went to look up to respond, her head rolled off her shoulders and she dematerialized. The Haddrill child ran horrified out of the barn, believing that the paranormal occurrences

The Haddrill farmhouse, currently serving as Revival Salon. *Author's photo.*

were a result of their father's ruthless actions. Let it be noted that these eerie occurrences still continue at the C-Pub today. In addition to Haddrill disturbing and destroying the Native American burial mound, the farm witnessed more deaths over the years.

Another legend associated with the property involves a young girl named Sara. It was an extremely early morning when a friend of the Haddrill family came by to help out at the farm and brought along their brood of children. While the adults were in the barn milking the cows, the family friend's nine-year-old daughter, Sara, and her siblings were playing in the field. As dairy farmers, the Haddrills valued every drop of milk their cows could produce and could not risk spoilage. After the adults completed the job, they speedily loaded the containers of fresh cream onto the wagon to take into town. As the driver of the wagon was going full speed ahead to make it into town ahead of schedule, he was not paying attention to what was in front of him and ran over little Sara. In a moment of panic, she was taken to the family homestead, where she was laid out. Every effort was taken to save her life, but she perished from the brutal injuries she endured.

The spirit of a playful little girl continues to be seen at the property. She is most likely climbing on rocks, sitting on the steps of the former homestead or running up and down the steps of the C-Pub. The sound of a young girl laughing and the *pitter-patter* of her small feet accompany the sightings. Occasionally, it sounds as if a ball is dropped down the steps, only for the bartenders to come out and find nothing out of the ordinary. The resident tailor at the village, Jason Womack, is one of many current staff members to have witnessed Sara's ghost on multiple occasions. A former maintenance man saw her as well and ended up resigning, unable to make sense of what he had seen. Visitors to the village who have seen her find her appearance rather hair-raising. Sara has been described as wearing a long, dark Victorian dress with her pin-straight dark hair in a chin-length bob. At a quick glance, she looks like any other child in a period costume, but upon closer inspection, she appears quite sickly, with an ashen face and eyes like two black pools.

When one of the Haddrill's sons, James, turned twenty-one, he rented a portion of the land from his father so he could begin farming it. Eight years after renting his father's property, at the age of twenty-nine, he purchased additional land and followed in his father's footsteps by making his home on the same land and by eventually marrying and having children of his own. Even though on the surface all appeared to be going well for James, he was regularly tormented with grim thoughts that he could not escape. On March 2, 1911, at the age of sixty-five years old, James took his own life while at his home on the property. His woebegone presence wasn't to appear until decades later after the property changed hands several times.

The Haddrill family owned the land until 1916, when they sold an amassed 600 acres of it, and the original structures, to William E. Scripps, heir of the *Detroit News* and, later, founder of WWJ News Radio and WWJ TV (later WDIV-TV). Scripps desired to pursue his passions in agriculture and aviation, so in that same year, he founded Wildwood Farm. He went on to buy more land, accumulating a total of 3,830 acres. Over the years, Scripps put up many buildings across the property and even built his own airfield atop it. Famed pilot Amelia Earhart even flew an experimental ice-glider at the airfield in 1929, only eight years before her mysterious disappearance.

After Scripps's passing in 1952, the massive property was divided up and sold off to different organizations. Entrepreneur Howard Keating Jr. purchased the former Wildwood Farm in 1967 and operated Keatington's Antique Village for a brief amount of time until its closure in the early 1980s due to a struggling economy. The property sat untouched for nearly a decade until Stan Aldridge came into ownership in 1991. With the goal of

Amelia Earhart in an experimental ice-glider at Wildwood Farm, Lake Orion, Michigan, March 1929. *Jim Orr of the Collections of The Henry Ford.*

opening a Christmas village like the one in Frankenmuth, he spent two years restoring the neglected property. In 2020, Stan's son, Keith, and his wife, Angie, purchased the village and repurposed it to support local businesses and host local events.

Sometime between the ownership of Howard Keating Jr. and Stan Aldridge, the C-Pub was born, and visitors to the village were ecstatic at the addition. But they were not prepared for the otherworldly sights they would behold while there. Customers would suspiciously spy a well-dressed older man wearing a tailcoat suit and a tall stovepipe hat making rounds through the pub. When Erin Schaefer of Lansing visited the pub for the first time with her family, she couldn't help but feel underdressed when she caught a glimpse of the well-dressed man. "I started to wonder if we had crashed a wedding reception or something. Here we all were in ratty old t-shirts and shorts, and this guy next to me was dressed to the nines." Oddly enough, the man never sat down, and after he would walk through the entire bar, he would swiftly turn and walk out the exit. After Erin saw the man again later that evening, she just assumed he was a staff member. "I noticed he was still walking around the pub hours later, so I just figured he must've worked there. Maybe there was a period themed costume party or something that we didn't know about." But weeks, months and even years later, whenever Erin would come back to visit, the man would still be there doing the same routine, never even bothering to say hello or acknowledge anyone around him. "I knew something wasn't right because it was like he didn't see anyone, and he just looked super melancholy. He was just in his own world, doing his own thing. And then, finally, after this great deal of time, I watched him evaporate into oblivion as he walked towards the liquor counter." The incident both fascinated and spooked Erin. "It was one of the craziest and coolest things I had ever seen in my life. I really thought he was a real person." A number of people believe this to be the spectral manifestation of James Haddrill. Other C-Pub customers have reported hearing a hysterical woman, endured uncomfortable cold spots and seen dark shadows hovering near them.

While the C-Pub is by far the most haunted liquor establishment on the property, the building housing Fourth Coast Ciderworks has its own ghost story. Located on the opposite end of the property from the C-Pub, it was historically used as a stable for workhorses. When the village was turned into a shopping center, the building was used as a clock shop for twenty-five years before becoming the hard cider bar it is today. At random times during the day, the clocks would all begin chiming one after the other until the entire structure was filled with the deafening, high-pitched sounds of various clock chimes. The proprietor of the shop would become infuriated, often storming up to Canterbury Village's owner and demanding he put a stop to the madness. However, the only thing that made the clocks stop was when the proprietor moved out, taking her clocks along with her.

The C-Pub has witnessed many ghost sightings through the years, including the spirit of James Haddrill. *Author's photo.*

Fourth Coast Ciderworks. *Author's photo.*

Everyone who visits Canterbury Village eventually has his or her own paranormal encounter to write home about. The next time you stop in for a drink, keep your eyes peeled and ears open. The person standing next to you might not even be real. And if you happen to make it in during the month of October, be sure to take a ghost tour with Terri Sharp, who conducts Canterbury Village Ghost Walks and co-operates a shop at the village. From the brightness of day to the tenebrosity of night, the many spirits of Canterbury Village never seem to rest.

WRAITHS OF THE RED LIGHT

CLIVE & AND DOT'S ANCHOR INN

1781 HEIGHTVIEW DRIVE
HOUGHTON LAKE, MI 48629

In 1914, Akin Bros. erected a multi-story building in Houghton Lake advertising groceries, meats, rooms and a restaurant. It was built atop an old lumbering settlement referred to as The Heights due to the elevation of the landscape. Despite Akin Bros. offering many services to the community, the establishment seemed to have an excessively high number of male clientele.

Sometime during this era, the boxing commission approved the bar as a venue to host boxing matches. The boxing that took place was more of an extreme sport rather than the boxing we are familiar with today, and men would use their bare fists to fight. Although it was uncommon during this time for Black and White combatants to compete in sports with each other, it had been allowed by the commission. One of the first biracial fights that took place in the bar resulted in a fatality. During the first bout, a Black man got hit below the belt, keeled over in the ring and died on the spot. His dead body was hurriedly whisked off to evade the eyes of spectators. When the government in Lansing got wind that the boxer died, it was outraged and promptly closed the commission down until an investigation was conducted. The conclusion was that the death was an accident and that malicious intent was not a factor. From this conclusion, they allowed the matches to continue, but the community was displeased by this type of death occurring in their hometown and used their voices to shut the commission down.

Akin Bros. only had the property for a brief amount of time before the business was bought out by Cliff Chapman, who changed the name to Cliff's Hotel.

As the years went on, high-profile gangsters like Al Capone and later Jimmy Hoffa began frequenting the location looking for a good time. During Prohibition, the notorious Purple Gang began smuggling alcohol into the establishment by way of underground tunnels, and the building became a hangout spot for some of Michigan's most heinous criminals. They would partake in high-stakes gambling and dogfighting and get intoxicated in the basement, and at the end of the night, they would follow the red light to the upper level seeking the attention of a woman. But the Purple Gang was known to leave nothing but trouble and death in its wake.

The first suspected murder in the building was a grisly sight to behold. A thirty-year-old man had bet too much money while in the gambling den and was unable to pay back an outstanding debt. The man who was owed the money came up and stabbed him in the gut, drawing the knife upward to sever his internal organs until he lay drowning in a pool of his own blood. These types of violent murders in relation to debts owed were, unfortunately, a rather normal occurrence among Purple Gang members. The ladies of the night were also targeted for physical abuse as victims of circumstance.

After Marie Yon (later Best) purchased the property, she became the madam and was in charge for many years. She was very protective over her girls and even gained the nickname "Mother Goose," as she would sit perched in the middle booth of the lounge observing all interactions between the girls and their clients with a watchful eye.

While Marie did look out for the girls as though they were her own children, brutality was an inevitable part of the job. Occasionally, some of the women would be killed if they did not consent to what was being done to them. Two ladies were thought to have died of natural causes based on historical documentation, but their deaths were believed to be anything but natural. The women were thought to be victims of smothering and strangulation, done at the hands of a married man in the late hours of the night. Based on the evidence, it's inferred that he killed these women because they knew too much; it's also surmised that he paid off the coroners to paint both deaths as unintentional. In the mornings, when these women were found dead in their beds, it was a heart-rending sight for Marie, who felt as though she lost family. One of the victims was a twenty-six-year-old woman referred to as "Elizabeth." Nothing was easy for girls in "the life."

Working girls were also forced to give birth in their assigned rooms since there wasn't a nearby hospital. This would lead to barbaric abortions with sharp tools and stillborn babies. Numerous babies were buried on the property in unmarked graves. Some of the women were deeply traumatized by these situations and the continual catering to the needs of such depraved men that they would commit suicide to escape their depressing reality. The twelve rooms upstairs would continue to bear witness to sufferings such as these for many years.

It is purported that an orphaned and impoverished teenager called "Virginia" was sent to the property to work and became impregnated by a client. Her baby did not make it and was one of many buried on site. It is believed that Virginia still roams the inn looking for her lifeless infant.

Evenings at the hotel were busy, with destitute schoolteachers looking for a way to make some quick cash off the backs of lustful men. One of those teachers was thought to be Flossie Kane, who taught at Houghton Lake School in the 1950s, as her class record books are stashed in what is presumed to be her designated room to this day.

The establishment's run with prostitution came to a screeching halt in 1985 when Savo ("Sam") and Jela Stajic became proprietors. The Stajics operated their business for twenty-six years, and then the business changed hands once more.

In 2011, Ronda Spears's parents, Clive and Dorothy ("Dot") Clymer, bought the historical building, as Clive had always desired to own a bar and renamed it Clive & Dot's Anchor Inn. Ronda was immediately hired in the first year to be the business manager with the support of her husband, Jason. Shortly after the Spearses began renovations on the building, they figured out that they were among incorporeal beings. Sadly, not long after purchasing the bar, Clive's dreams were cut short when he died of an illness at age eighty-one. Ronda wanted to honor her father's aspirations and take the burden of caring for a business off her mother, so she and her husband agreed to take up more responsibility.

Jason, a nonbeliever in the paranormal, began being sexually harassed by Emily, a flirtatious female spirit clad in red lingerie and fire engine red lips who even went as far as following him home one night. Ronda was shocked when she got an unsettling phone call one evening from Jason in which he pleaded, "You need to get home this instant; there's a strange woman in our house." All in good time, Ronda would become well acquainted with all of the spirits at the inn, but her own surprising paranormal encounter would come about one month into renovations.

One day, Ronda made her way up to the second floor alone in search of some items. Other than being used for storage by Sam, when he owned the place, the upstairs was like a time capsule, having been untouched for thirty years. Ronda stood in the center hallway searching for artifacts relating to the building's history as she gripped her illuminated flashlight in her right hand. Shining the light at the end of the hallway, toward the entrance, she was surprised to see another person staring back at her. A short and stout older lady with Lucille Ball red hair stood frozen in the center doorway transfixed by what was going on in front of her. She didn't say much of anything, but her expressive eyes followed Ronda's every move as if to say, *What are you doing here?* Before Ronda could even ask her name, the woman dissipated into the air.

"Do you know anyone associated with the building that has bright red hair?" Ronda asked Sam the following morning after detailing her paranormal encounter. "Yes, I do," he answered without hesitation. "I bought the property from a red-haired lady by the name of Marie Best." This information was enough to help propel Ronda forward in her search for more answers.

Ronda went back upstairs and began rifling through the many boxes that cluttered the hallway until she came across a stack of photographs. As Ronda began flipping through the photos, she stopped dead when she got to one of an older woman wearing a tight black dress with her bright-red hair in short ringlets. The corners of the lady's mouth were upturned into a slight smile as she hovered a little knife over the top of a cake. "Oh my God!" Ronda exclaimed. "That's her! That's who I saw!"

Whenever time permitted, Ronda would continue going through the boxes, coming across a phony cosmetology license printed on the back of a real estate sign that worked to lead men upstairs under the guise of a "shave and haircut." After Ronda began decorating the upstairs rooms with some of her findings, Marie's spirit began appearing downstairs in the lounge in the same booth she sat in when she was alive. Her eyes repeatedly scanned the perimeter of the room like a watchdog, making sure that her girls are still safe. Despite Marie being the one in charge, she's not the only one who makes her rounds at the inn.

One bartender who worked at a neighboring bar just across the street from the Anchor Inn told Ronda that after business hours, she would regularly see a young pale-haired apparition in a light-colored dress standing in the upstairs window. Whenever she would leave work for the night, she felt compelled to look up and would always see the girl looking back at her.

Right: Marie Best. *Ronda Spears of Clive & Dot's Anchor Inn.*

Below: A phony cosmetology license printed on the back of a real estate sign that worked to lead men upstairs under the guise of a "shave and haircut." *Ronda Spears of Clive & Dot's Anchor Inn.*

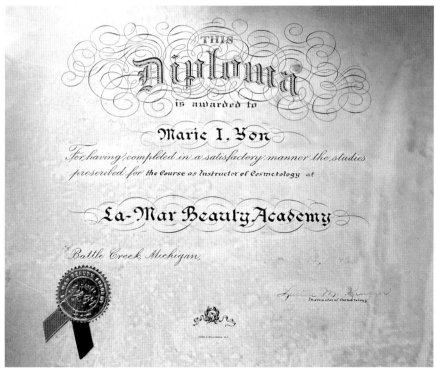

After a week or two of seeing the apparition, the bartender decided to wave at the girl, and the apparition never appeared in the window again. But little did Ronda know that the remaining souls at the inn would take a liking to her spiritually sensitive son.

One late night after closing, Ronda's son was driving home when he realized that he left his cellphone on the end of the bar. He wasn't too far away, so he swung the car around and headed back to the inn. After unlocking the main door, he dashed to the end of the bar, but then something caught his attention. A young lady was standing in the little hallway located just beyond the other end of the bar. She appeared no older than the age of sixteen and matched the description of the apparition upstairs in the window with shoulder-length blond hair and a pale frock. Ronda's son had stepped forward just enough to grab his cellphone when the figure began walking aimlessly toward him. Totally shaken by the experience, he booked it out of the inn and drove home, leaving a trail of dust in his midst.

The most aggressive spirit at the bar is referred to as "Big John" and is believed to be a former bouncer of the bar. He seems to get the most enjoyment out of tormenting women. In early 2012, female staff began to complain that they could feel and hear someone breathing heavily down their necks and into their ears while they were standing alone at the bar. As a result, closing up shop alone was out of the question for them. They would shut the bar down early in an attempt to avoid confrontation with the hostile spirit and get the hell out of the building before twilight. Today, female customers who visit the bar will sometimes be subjected to his unpleasant antics. Big John has previously manifested in photographs as a burly shadow figure, but Ronda's son has been the only person he has appeared to in full physical form.

When Big John appeared to Ronda's son, he manifested in the same hallway as the young female spirit, but he appeared as a tall, heavyset man in a flannel shirt and denim pants. The hallway behind him also seemed to be stuck in a time warp, as Ronda's framed photographs no longer lined the present-day drywall. Nothing but pale slats of wood surrounded the figure, and as he vanished, so did the scene behind him. Ronda found this particularly chilling, indicating that the entire building was initially created of blonde wood and that the surviving wood in the structure, such as the booths, have darkened due to age, cigar smoke and various other elements.

As soon as energy readers and paranormal investigators got wind of the inn being a portal for paranormal activity, they began flooding through the

A drawing by Brian Danhausen of the spirit that appeared to him at the inn. *Ronda Spears of Clive & Dot's Anchor Inn with permission from Brian Danhausen.*

doors hoping to have their own experience. Brian Danhausen, a spiritual medium and energy painter from the Detroit metro area, was one of them.

Brian spent the whole day at the inn doing readings for guests, but there was one individual he could not get out of his head. When the event ended, Brian made a beeline for Ronda, handing her a small piece of paper and, said, "This gentleman came to me. I drew him. He's here." When Ronda looked down at the paper, she could not believe her eyes. There in her hands was a drawing of a Black man in Edwardian dress with the words *African American, beat, blood, bruise* and *man* surrounding the sketch. Immediately, Ronda knew that Brian interacted with the boxer who was fatefully killed only a few steps away from where they stood. The most astonishing thing of all was that Brian never knew the history of the boxer because the information regarding his death had never been readily available to the public. Although Ronda was truly impressed by Brian's spiritual abilities, there would be an even larger surprise in store for her.

Ronda and her son went to pick up a few bottles of alcohol at the store to restock the bar, and a few of those bottles were of the Scotch whisky known as Cutty Sark. After checking out, they loaded up the vehicle, drove straight to the inn, replaced and discarded any empty bottles at the bar and put the additional liquor in storage. Over the next few weeks, customers began approaching Ronda about a man who was smoking a pipe at the end of the bar and enjoying some liquor on the rocks, nearest to the front entrance.

Upset to hear that someone was smoking in her non-smoking establishment, Ronda would run over to the bar and not see anyone there. She would then reply, "Well, what did the man look like?" Each time someone described the man they saw, they said he resembled Clark Gable with dark, slicked-back hair, a distinguished mustache and a sleek suit. All was just a minor inconvenience for Ronda until she realized, on top of everything else, that the alcohol inside the bottle of Cutty Sark was mysteriously vanishing. This truly puzzled her because hardly anyone ever ordered Cutty Sark, but she kept it on hand for a few diehards. Finally, one day as she was hanging up family photos, she came across the photo of a man who fit the description of the man smoking the pipe at the bar. It was her late grandfather, Clive Clymer Sr.! And in life, he sure did love his pipe! But who in the world was drinking all the dang Cutty Sark?

Ronda excitedly relayed to her mother that she had solved the mystery of the smoking man but went on to explain that the volume of alcohol was rapidly diminishing out of a big bottle that she just got from the store, despite the lack of requests for it. "What kind of alcohol is it?" her mom asked inquisitively. "Cutty Sark," Ronda replied nonchalantly,

Clive Clymer Sr. *Ronda Spears of Clive & Dot's Anchor Inn.*

unsure why it mattered. A smile grew across her mother's face. "Cutty Sark was your grandfather's favorite."

Ronda ended up having a good long talk with her grandfather about drinking the Cutty Sark, and it hasn't happened since. She did, however, refer him to the bar down the road, so she does wonder if the other business goes through Cutty Sark bottles like they're water.

Family sure can drive us crazy, but Ronda feels grateful to have them near her in spirit, along with all the other wandering souls. Thankfully, her father has made his presence known at the inn too, and it's obvious that he's proud of what she's done with the place. This comforting presence has helped Ronda to accept the assemblage of spirits that join her at the inn. "In the past, businesses would have swept this sort of thing under the rug. There's a lot of paranormal shenanigans that go on here. Stuff happens here pretty much every single day. Instead of shying away from it, I thought to myself, *Why not just embrace it?*" Between hosting various paranormal community events, historical paranormal tours and running an annual haunt, it appears Ronda has done just that.

FAMILIAL PHANTOMS

ABICK'S BAR

3500 GILBERT STREET
DETROIT, MI 48210

The two-story brown brick building at the corner of Gilbert and Dennis Streets in the heart of southwest Detroit doesn't look drastically different from other structures in the area. But one step inside and it's like you've been transported back in time. For more than a century, the building predominantly served as a neighborhood bar, gathering place and home for the Abick/Soviak family and their descendants. Portions of it also served as a barbershop, shoeshine, icehouse and temporary classroom for new immigrants. After the reins of ownership were passed down to the sixth-generation descendant of the family, Eric Lakeman, he never imagined in a million years his family would be watching him from beyond the grave.

In the early 1900s, eastern European families were flocking to Detroit, mainly to get jobs in the growing auto industry but also to establish their own businesses. Many had come from the Carpathian Mountains. John Wasielewski, a Polish immigrant, was one of those people. On July 13, 1907, John visited the office of the Detroit fire marshal to apply for a building permit. His request was granted, and he began building what would later become Abick's Bar. While the bar was being constructed, he operated a saloon just across the way from the site. Luckily, the Stroh's Brewing Company agreed to underwrite the costs associated with running the business and provided installation of the bar so long as it exclusively sold Stroh's beer.

Exterior of Abick's and Barber Shop (present-day cigar lounge), circa 1918. *Eric Lakeman and Kit Lindamood of Abick's Bar.*

Through the years, even more of his family began immigrating to the States, including his dear nephew John Benske, who arrived in 1910 with his first wife, Julia, and inherited the bar upon his arrival. Soon other family members and newfound friends were showing up to help out at the bar. The first bartender the couple hired was a handsome young man from Prague by the name of George Abick.

Before the 1920s, Benske's nephew, Michael Urda, immigrated to the United States from Austrian Poland (Galicia) to help his uncle with the bar and was followed by his sister, Katarina (Kasia), who later Americanized her name to Katherine.

When George and Katherine locked eyes with each other, sparks flew, and it was like no one else was in the room. As days turned into weeks and weeks turned into months, Katherine and George found themselves getting closer and closer until he realized that he couldn't live without her and requested her hand in marriage. In 1919, the duo tied the knot in a large ceremony and were given the bar as a wedding present. They wasted no time in starting their family. By October 4, 1923, after having three sons—George Jr., John and Walter ("Podge")—the Abicks welcomed their fourth child and only daughter into the family, Marie ("Manya").

Podge and Manya out front before going off to World War II. *Eric Lakeman and Kit Lindamood of Abick's Bar.*

From a very young age, the children were put to work at the bar, with the hopes that they would someday be able to take over for their parents. This proved helpful when George Sr. passed away in 1935 and the Abick boys went off to fight in World War II. Through all the trials and tribulations, Manya held down the fort with her mother and learned firsthand what running a bar was all about.

Manya went on to marry a debonair gentleman by the name of William Soviak and had two children, her youngest a daughter by the name of Marie ("Mamie").

After Manya's mother died in 1964 due to a horrific car accident, Manya and Podge became co-owners of the bar and continued the Abick tradition of goodwill in the neighborhood by providing food to veterans and the needy, offering business referrals and providing community support in times of hardship. Manya and Podge were hopeful that someday their children would fill their shoes, but it never came to be. When Mamie gave birth to her only son, Eric, he worked alongside Manya and Podge for years until both of them passed away from old age, both living into their early nineties.

For most of his life, Eric, a reserved and pragmatic curmudgeon of sorts, adamantly refused to admit that the building he called his work and home was haunted. After years of struggling to explain away the poltergeist activity with logical explanations, he continued to grapple with the fact that most of the activity has been centered on him. When friends, such as bartenders Kit Lindamood and Jessica Trail, began spending more time in the building, they could not help but notice it as well.

In late 2019, a paranormal investigation requested by one of the local Prohibition tour companies was allowed by Abick's. Eric, along with two investigators, gathered in the main bar, while the rest of the people split up into investigative groups on the property. One investigator was interviewing Eric about his experiences, while another wandered the perimeter of the room as he operated an SLS-XCam (a Structured Light Sensor device that helps individuals to see data that the human eye cannot, presenting that visual

Katherine (front) and Manya holding down the fort while the boys were off to war. *Eric Lakeman and Kit Lindamood of Abick's Bar.*

data in the form of a stick figure). As Eric was sharing stories of personal loss, the investigator panned the SLS-XCam over toward him and watched as a figure began manifesting on the device in the chair directly next to Eric. The figure seemed to be consoling Eric, with its arm outstretched, soothingly rubbing his back. While this approach was heartwarming, nothing tugged at Eric's heartstrings more than being shown the footage—to his disbelief, the figure's legs were double-crossed.

When Eric was a child, nothing impressed him more than how intricately his thin mother was able to weave her spindly legs together. He fondly remembers sitting around the bar shooting the breeze with his mother and grandmother as his mom did "the leg thing," while his mother giggled at his childhood wonder and amazement over it. Unfortunately, Eric only got to enjoy thirteen short years with his mother before she tragically passed away from terminal cancer at the age of forty-five. After his mother's passing, he made his home in the upstairs apartment his grandfather used to occupy, just across the hall from his grandmother, entirely unaware that just five to six months later, he would be seeing his mother again.

Eric was sitting at his newly assembled desk hutch in the room next to his bedroom. He had been chatting on the phone with his girlfriend when, out of the blue, his mother appeared to him. She was hovering in the corner of the room next to the laundry basket about six feet away from where he was sitting. From the knees down, she was totally invisible, but from the knees up she looked as physically real as anyone else.

Eric was so caught off guard by the experience that he did not want to believe it was real and could barely bring himself to look at the sight of the floating apparition. He put his head down and continued talking on the phone hoping it would just go away, but when he glanced back over, the ghost of his mother was still there. She lingered around for almost three whole minutes before evaporating. After this sight had dissipated, Eric raced downstairs in search of his grandmother to tell her what just occurred.

After the sighting, Eric tried to forget about it and attempted to make his living quarters more comfortable and inviting. He put up more furniture and decorated shelving units with childhood possessions, including draping a belt with a heavy mac tools belt buckle he received from his estranged father across the top of one of his mother's bookshelves that was inside the closet.

About three years later, Eric lay sleeping in his bed when he was awakened by an unusual knocking sound coming from inside of his bedroom closet. He looked around blurry-eyed, but the sound stopped and Eric fell back to sleep. About fifteen minutes later, Eric woke up again as the sound became a bit louder. Thinking it was perhaps his mother, he said, "Please stop. I understand you're here and I'm trying to sleep." Just as Eric said that, he was overcome by an unbearable feeling of dread. The loving warmth of his beloved home was now filled with a heavy and abnormal weight in the air. Eric realized that his mother's spirit was no longer present. The sound reoccurred every fifteen to twenty minutes until Eric reached his breaking point. Enraged, he yelled, "Knock it off, dammit! I said I'm trying to sleep! I'm done with it!" At this point, severe banging ensued inside the closet. Eric flew up from the bed, threw the covers off himself and onto the floor and ran over to the closet, whipping the door open. There he observed as the heavy belt buckle smacked repeatedly against the side of the bookcase with no breeze in sight. Between experiencing an array of emotions from anger to shock to fear, he grabbed the belt and buckle and whipped it across the room. He then grabbed his pillow, blanket and gun and made his way downstairs to the back room, where he slept between his grandmother's lower-level bedroom and the women's bathroom. The next afternoon, Eric's grandmother broke the news to him that she had received a call that his father had died.

As Eric grew older and began living with his fiancée in the apartment, they both could not help but notice how their little dog, Odie, would always lock eyes on the closet. The two often laughed it off, joking that Odie was looking at the ghost of Manya's childhood dog, Moxie. One day, while Eric's fiancée was at work, he set up a mirrored vanity set for her in the closet—coincidentally in the same spot as mom's bookshelf with the banging belt buckle. Over the course of the night, the dog continued to become more agitated by what he was seeing inside the closet. The next morning, the couple woke up to find that the closet door was closed, and the vanity had moved overnight. It was placed in front of the door, which could not be opened, as if to say, *Keep out!*

During the 2019 investigation, the investigator who was operating the SLS-XCam was back in the cigar room when he caught a figure crawling up the wall in the left-hand corner of the room, across from the bathroom and into the tin ceiling. The room above it? The closet.

Eric was spooked yet not surprised by this evidence. "That damn closet has been the bane of my existence since I was a kid."

The paranormal activity certainly amped up after the death of both Podge and Manya. Kit and Eric discussed celebrating Manya's legacy every year on her birthday after her passing, as she was revered like royalty and was a treasured icon in the community for many years. People even took bus tours in Detroit to come see Abick's matriarch! Much to the surprise of others, Manya was quite a demure person. Even decades after Prohibition, Manya refused to discuss it, only saying, "The boys took care of us." She was also very humble and felt uncomfortable with people fawning over her. Despite knowing this, Kit wanted to do something kind and assumed that hosting this annual celebration would go off without a hitch. How wrong she was.

When the day came, Kit purchased various desserts, including a large cake that bore the words "Happy Birthday, Manya," and placed it on a table in the back room just to the right of the kitchenette. A caterer who was preparing to grill behind the building came in to grab something and exited out the back door, which filled the room with an obnoxious metal-on-metal screech. Upon his exit, Kit was alone in the building and returned to the bar to stock up for the party. Then, without warning, she was startled by the crashing sound of glass shattering. In shock, she ran into the back room and couldn't believe her eyes. A vase that was filled with marbles and dried flowers that had previously been sitting on top of the microwave clear across the room was now smashed at the foot of the cake table. Kit knew that no one had entered or exited either the front or back doors at the time this occurred and took this as a sign to never throw Manya another birthday party as long as she was there.

Many have reported seeing Manya in shadow form heading to and from the kitchen and resting in her designated chair located in the back room near the microwave, as well as the end barstool closest to the beer cooler. However, the most prevalent spirit at the bar is Podge.

Podge was always headstrong in life and has become even more so in death. Due to his military service in the U.S. Navy, Podge never wavered on being meticulous about the proper way to clean. This was especially the case when it came to making sure that the floors were spotless. He strongly believed that the floor should be mopped in tight figure-eight swirls until every last speck of dirt was obsolete. While Eric was growing up, there were many instances in which Eric didn't mop the floor up to Podge's standards and was sent right back in to do it again. If the floor didn't shine like sparkling crystal, the job wasn't complete. He still lingers around, making sure that the bar is in tip-top shape.

In 2019, Abick's closed for a few days during the week of Christmas so Eric and his friends could do a deep clean, polish the floor and varnish the bar. They started with the flooring, as that involved lifting a few of the ridiculously heavy, poured marble terrazzo-top tables and putting them face-down on the bar. They desperately desired to get that strenuous chore out of the way. After the tables were atop the bar, everyone left except neighbor and family friend Chavo. Eric and his friend spent the entire day putting several layers of clear coat on the floor in order to achieve that glassy shine that Podge found so satisfying. After starting in the morning and working all the way up until ten o'clock at night, Eric sleepily proclaimed, "That is good enough!" He then ordered a pizza for a late dinner and went to sit back in the cigar room located just behind the bar to visit with Chavo, so the two men could eat and rest their weary bodies. After taking a bite of their pizza, the two men were jolted by a tremendous *thud* coming from the bar.

Knowing that they were alone in the bar and horrified that something expensive had been broken, Eric and Chavo emerged wide-eyed from the cigar room, wondering what had caused such a commotion. After scanning the room, both men took a step back in shock when they realized that one of those extremely heavy marble tables was no longer on the bar but had moved all the way to the back bar, more than four feet in distance, and was wedged into a cubby hole. "The bar is majorly slanted from over a hundred years of wear. If that table had been sliding off, it would have crashed into the small glass door cooler beneath the bar. Instead, the table had entirely relocated upwards," Eric said, taking this as a sign from his great-uncle Podge that taking shortcuts around the bar was simply unacceptable. "He

Manya's English mastiff, Shadow. *Eric Lakeman and Kit Lindamood of Abick's Bar.*

made it very clear to me that night that he wanted another coat applied, so I sucked up how I was feeling and did it. He took a lot of pride in his bar, and I want to continue making him proud."

Unfortunately for Podge, Manya's English mastiff, Shadow, still haunts the bar as well, scuffing up the flooring with his massive paws. Shadow was appropriately named after following Manya everywhere, including lying at her feet while she sat at the bar. Nowadays, unsuspecting customers who sit at the end barstool may feel Shadow's 160-pound body smash against their legs. The pressure behind the sensation has nearly knocked a few folks to the floor. Occasionally, Kit has also heard the unmistakable sound of Shadow dragging his paws against the floor, an indicator that he wants to go run around outside.

Jessica frequently helps out alone and will bring her dog, Oswald, a Basset hound German Shepherd mix, with her for safety. When at the bar, he never fails to stand in the doorway to the back room, growl and bark loudly at the little hallway near the ladies' restroom. But it's not Shadow that causes Oswald to go crazy—it's often good ol' Podge riling up the canine.

It's safe to say that the whole family is spiritually together at Abick's, accompanied by their furry friends. This was made very apparent during the ghost hunt when the investigators asked, "Are you here?" and a spirit replied, "*Si siempre*," which means "Yes, always" in Spanish. Why the reply in Spanish? No one can be sure, but perhaps it's because Abick's is a melting pot of cultures founded by Polish/eastern Europeans in the center of Detroit's Mexicantown. And while all the spirits are friendly, apart from the closet dweller, Eric has no plans to intentionally disrupt their peace. "This is their home and will always be their home. I'm just the caretaker here."

Graveyard Mayhem at the Grotto

Dexter Beer Grotto

8059 Main Street
Dexter, MI 48130

Manager Phil Blass knew that something wasn't quite right when an overwrought regular came rushing up to him begging him to come check out something strange in the women's bathroom. That regular wasn't just anyone. It was Jen DeGregorio, an upstanding citizen in Washtenaw County and someone who had formed close friendships with the owners and staff since the bar's opening on July 2, 2014. Blass had no reason not to believe Jen and promptly followed her to the single-person ladies' restroom, where she pointed out an upside-down flyer. After the COVID-19 shutdown, Jen began sensing a presence in the building that she hadn't noticed previously. She had several of her own paranormal encounters and decided to ask the entity privately for a sign of confirmation while in the bathroom. In the short time frame between asking for a sign and coming back to use the restroom again, she noticed that the once right-side-up flyer was now hanging upside-down. Where on earth did this spirit come from? Many speculate that it came just a stone's throw away in Scio Village.

Near the intersection of Zeeb Road and Huron River Drive, shrouded by overgrown land, is the historic half-acre Scio Cemetery, which has been crudely neglected for many years. The dead have been long forgotten, and their gravestones were stolen and desecrated by unruly teenagers, as well

Jen DeGregorio. *Jen DeGregorio.*

as eroded by the elements. This once sacred place became frequented by troublemakers and heavy drinkers, who treated the area more like a landfill than hallowed ground. These graves belonged to pioneers of Scio Township, and today not even a marker has been erected in memory of these lost souls who were buried between the years of 1838 and 1864.

Around the time that Scio Village was established, in 1832, Captain Elias Hayes, a naval officer who had served in the War of 1812, settled in Scio Township on Dexter-Ann Arbor Road. Upon Hayes's death, a thorn tree was planted in his honor, although his final resting place was in Kalkaska County. The tree grew and grew, and after a considerable time it split into two giant separate trunks. Joseph W. Seymour, one of the village's earliest settlers, died in 1840, and over time his headstone became embedded between the trunks of the massive tree. His headstone was ultimately pried out and stolen. Due to urban legend, many believed Joseph to be a warlock or vampire based on how the tree grew to frame his tombstone.

At the end of the 1930s, Walter Laubengayer of Ann Arbor purchased the farm, and his wife worked diligently to restore the cemetery. However, the property continued to change hands until the township took over the cemetery and labeled it as abandoned by the State Cemetery Association.

Despite repeated attempts by the Dexter Area Historical Society to restore the cemetery and get others excited about restoration efforts, no one seemed to care. Time hadn't been kind to the constantly decaying grounds, and eventually any attempt at restoration became a lost cause.

In addition to the abandoned cemetery, the village of Scio fought hard to become the most populated village in Scio Township against both Dexter and Delhi. It failed. In 1841, both Scio and Delhi were nearly wiped out entirely when railroad tracks were implemented in Dexter. Various industries and businesses in both tiny villages tanked, while Dexter expanded and was given all the glory. Legend has it that the forsaken spirits of the Scio Cemetery have descended on Dexter, seeking their revenge, and cursed the very land that Dexter sits on today, with Main Street as their primary target.

Main Street has been the main business district in Dexter since the early days, and over the years, it has suffered wicked devastation from fires. In November 1844, twelve storefronts on the north side of Main Street were turned to ashes. And again, in April 1877, a row of structures was destroyed on the south side of Main Street. The worst part of all? The store owners had to wait until fire trucks came from Ann Arbor, as there was no fire department in Dexter at the time of the fires. Fortunately, there were no

MAIN ST. DEXTER, MICH. 121-12

Opposite: A thorn tree grows around Joseph Seymour's headstone at the Scio Cemetery. ©*1949 MLive Media Group/Ann Arbor News, all rights reserved, used with permission.*

Above: View of commercial buildings on Main Street in Dexter, Michigan, date unknown. *Burton Historical Collection, Detroit Public Library.*

Left: The exterior of the Dexter Beer Grotto. *Author's photo.*

known casualties, yet many people began reporting paranormal happenings at different locations along Main Street. One of those locations was none other than the property that now houses the Dexter Beer Grotto.

The Dexter Beer Grotto was founded by the Mekas family, who have been contenders in the restaurant industry for decades. Although they are from Detroit, they have established businesses all over the state of Michigan. When they turned what used to be the old Dexter Pharmacy into a beer-lovers' paradise, with select ciders and wines available, they never imagined in a million years that their place would be considered haunted. And flyers turning upside down certainly wasn't the worst of it.

During the pandemic, the Mekases decided to entirely remodel their bar, even going as far as moving all the draft lines. Around this time, Jen offered to assist with social media management to get people excited about the upcoming changes to the bar and even raised $10,000 for the staff who couldn't work during the shutdown. Needless to say, she began spending a lot of time there in order to get photographs and advertise different menu offerings. But each time she would go to use the restroom, she was overcome by a strange feeling. After trying a few different types of wine, Jen felt the urge to use the bathroom. She got up and made her way there, where she attempted to open the door, but quickly realized that it was locked. She could see the dark silhouette of a woman moving around inside through the frosted glass on the door but just assumed that someone else was in there. After a line started to develop, Jen's patience began wearing a little thin. She went up to jiggle the lock as if to say, *Hey, other people have to use the bathroom too!*, and found that, miraculously, the door was unlocked and no one was inside. This began happening on such a regular basis that she had hoped to find the culprit.

Talking to other staff members, Jen learned that she was not alone in her experiences and that other female staff have reported similar happenings. One incident involved the automatic paper towel dispenser inside the ladies' bathroom. One of the bartenders who was newly hired at the time went to clean the restroom at the end of the night and discovered that every single paper towel in the stack had been activated and was placed in an immaculate pile on the floor. To say she was befuddled by the occurrence would be an understatement. Despite referring to the elusive figure as the "shadow man," staff strongly believe that the entity is female. Visitors who've encountered the figure believe so as well.

A University of Michigan student went to the Dexter Beer Grotto one evening for a drink with some classmates. She had spent a good forty-five minutes to an hour conversing over drinks when she was hit with the need to use the bathroom. The door wasn't locked, so she sauntered in and took a seat on the toilet, which faces away from the sink and is separated by a small wall. She began to hear water dripping. She didn't pay much attention to it, as she thought the faucet was just leaky or hadn't been turned off all the way by the previous person who used it. Suddenly, the student could hear what sounded like someone thoroughly washing their hands. It ran through her mind that she didn't lock the door, so she turned around, partially covering herself, and yelled, "Excuse me, I'm in here!" Shockingly, the water turned off, but the student began to hear the faint sound of a woman ululating directly behind her.

Re-creating shadows from behind the frosted-glass window of the women's bathroom door to get a sense of what Jen experienced. *Author's photo.*

The student yanked her pants up in a hurry and ran around the wall, discovering that she was alone—or so she thought. She dismissed the sound as coming from the bar and proceeded to wash her hands; suddenly, she saw something weird appear behind her in the mirror. A translucent form about the size of a basketball that resembled the texture of a bubble hovered over her left shoulder for a few seconds before seeming to dissipate into the mirror itself. In a state of confusion, she brought her face closer to inspect the residue, but it only looked like water. Like magic, a ghoulish face appeared in the mirror just centimeters from her own. The student jumped back in fright, but after realizing that nothing was there, she second-guessed herself, thinking that she was just drunk and had conjured the vision up in her mind.

After splashing some cool water on her face to sober up, she grabbed a paper towel to blot off the excess moisture so she could return to her table. As she took one final glance at herself in the mirror, she could unmistakably make out that there was the hazy face of a woman looking back at her. Even though the outline of her face was quite undefined, her facial features were distinctly ominous, with sunken, empty eyes and large decayed teeth that projected out of her skeletal and atrophied jaw. At this point, the student knew for sure that she was not imagining the image inside the mirror and barreled out of the bathroom, detailing the horrifying sight to her friends.

If you find yourself at the Dexter Beer Grotto, just be aware that the eerie apparition continues to lurk in the ladies' restroom, creating mischief every chance it gets. It's likely she's trying to scare away customers and hurt business, but little does she know there is such a thing as dark tourism nowadays. While it's horrible that her final resting place has been disregarded by so many in society, there are many morbidly curious individuals who would give anything to come face to face with the bloodcurdling apparition, just as the student did.

BREWED TO THE BITTER END

JAMESPORT BREWING COMPANY

410 SOUTH JAMES STREET
LUDINGTON, MI 49431

W e shall meet soon, my love," a young expectant mother said tenderly as she cradled her rounded belly in her hands and smiled. Although it was the Victorian age and becoming a mother had many challenges, she could not help but feel excited about the little bundle of joy growing inside her. The joyous woman decided that she needed to step outside for a bit of fresh air. She slipped on a jacket for warmth and ambled gleefully to the stairwell, where she began her descent to the sidewalk below. On the way down, she lost her footing and tragically plummeted to her death. For more than one hundred years, this tale was passed on by locals in Ludington as a true story with sadly very little verifiable documentation, presumably because it would deter potential customers from wanting to stay at the hotel. But after the unfortunate lady's death, the building that currently houses the Jamesport Brewing Company took on a life all its own. It is said that this grieving mother haunts the location due to the incredible loss she suffered, always wishing she could go back and fix the fatal error that led to the demise of both her and her unborn child. She also attempts to keep others safe from the same misfortune. Remarkable amounts of paranormal activity have been reported since the tragedy, but it only began being documented in recent years, especially during times when the business was closed to the public.

The stairwell where the young mother is thought to have fallen to her death. *Jennifer Tooman of Jamesport Brewing Company.*

It is suspected that the young woman was a guest at the Central House Hotel at the time of her death, which was established on the second story of the structure two years after the Red Andrews Saloon was built in 1890. The whole building originally consisted of six linked storefronts and was called the Jamesport Center, with the hotel and bar being built first. Starting in 1905, the other four storefronts would go on to serve as various industries for more than 120 years, in addition to providing housing for employees of the Star Watch Case Company, which was formerly located on Rath Street.

The saloon was built by prominent architect and builder August Tiedmann at the request of two brothers who emigrated from Sweden, Andrew "Red" and Axel Johnson. During the logging boom in western Michigan, the saloon became a staple among weary sailors who traversed the Great Lakes and sought a place to come unwind after their arduous journeys. After the hotel had been built, it gave the sailors a place to stay after drinking themselves into a drunken stupor, but it also was utilized by people from all walks of life who sought a comfy place to lay their heads.

Jennifer "Jen" Tooman got involved at the Jamesport Brewing Company as a server in 2001 while she was going to college. While she found that she really loved the culture and fast-paced environment of the hospitality industry, she could not ignore the eerie and tragic stories that have been circulating around the facility for almost as long as it's been standing. Through hard work, she was promoted to a management role and worked full time as both a server and manager until 2009. Then, from 2009 to 2015, she worked only part-time at the company before taking a seven-year hiatus and eventually returning in the spring of 2022 with the title of business development manager. In her long duration of working for the company, Jen experienced a lot of strange phenomena that could not be easily explained.

One evening, after a long day of work, Jen along with two other employees fixed themselves a drink and sat down to reflect on their chaotic day. As the facility was closed, most of the lights were off, creating a serene and relaxing environment. As the three staff members sat around sipping their beverage of choice, they could hear the gentle clinking of glasses from one end of the bar to the other. It sounded as if someone was walking along the bar, pushing each glass against another as they went. As the sound made its way closer and closer to the employees, they all looked at one another in fright and left the building without saying a single word.

Staff grew accustomed to the minor inconveniences of doors opening on their own, seeing shadows alongside or behind their person, hearing their names whispered in their ears and phantom footsteps following their every move in all areas of the building. One of the employees who cleans the facility even resorted to wearing earplugs during her shifts, to drown out not only the loud sounds of the vacuum but also the bizarre noises that are believed to be of supernatural origin. However, one of the more hair-raising occurrences involved a door leading to a storage closet that is about twelve

Above: The glasses at the bar have been known to take on a life of their own. *Jennifer Tooman of Jamesport Brewing Company.*

Opposite, top: One of the glass growlers sitting high on the shelf flew off by itself and shattered. *Jennifer Tooman of Jamesport Brewing Company.*

Opposite, bottom: The Jamesport Brewing Company as it stands today. *Jennifer Tooman of Jamesport Brewing Company.*

feet off the main floor and can only be accessed by ladder. At the most unsuspecting of times, staff will notice that the door has been opened and then, a few days later, see that it has been closed, yet no ladder was utilized. It makes one question: Is the figure perpetuating the activity extremely tall? Is it floating up to open and close the door? Or is it crawling up and down the walls? Either way, the thought is quite disturbing.

Another chill-inducing occurrence that happened near the ceiling took place during the late summer of 2022. The closing bar manager was cleaning behind the bar when, out of nowhere, a glass growler that had been sitting high on a shelf above the back room appeared to have been thrown off and smashed into smithereens all over the floor. The shelf is another area of the building that could not be reached without the use of a ladder, and no one else, apart from the bar manager, was in the building at that time.

It's no doubt that the Jamesport Brewing Company has more than its fair share of haunted happenings, but there is one event in specific that bolsters fear unlike any other: being trapped alone inside the bathroom. In countless instances, people were getting locked inside the restrooms so often that management actually had to saw off the bottom of the full-sized stall doors to get the people out. At one time, a single-stall restroom was added upstairs, and within just a few days of it being open, someone got locked inside of it. As you can imagine, claustrophobia and anxiety set in as staff struggled to wedge a screwdriver underneath the door and instructed the confined individual to remove the hinges off the door so that they could get out. Many theorize that this is a way that the spirit helps to keep others safe, with the mentality that if one can't leave the room, one certainly won't be able to fall down a staircase, as they once did.

There is a strong belief that the spirit haunting the building is likely that of the deceased mother-to-be, and employees began referring to the entity as "Pilar." As far as the staff is aware, no one with the name Pilar has any connections to the property, but they attempted to make light of a very dark situation by giving the spirit a more eclectic feminine name.

The paranormal activity at the Jamesport Brewing Company doesn't seem to be slowing down anytime soon, but Jen is hopeful that some of the activity will be captured by newly installed security cameras. The next time you end up on the western side of Michigan in the entrancing harbor town of Ludington, prioritize making the Jamesport Brewing Company a stop for delicious food and drinks, and you may possibly encounter the ghost of Pilar on your visit.

The Apple Doesn't Fall Far from the Scream

Robinette's Apple Haus & Winery

3142 4 Mile Road Northeast
Grand Rapids, MI 49525

Michigan is the third-largest producer of apples in the nation, with 775 family-run apple orchards. So, the fact that Robinette's Apple Haus & Winery in Grand Rapids has built a stellar reputation as one of the best apple orchards in the state of Michigan is quite impressive. Robinette's has proven for more than a century to be infallible and invaluable to Grand Rapids' community. The orchard, which spans 125 acres, boasts forty different types of apples and a variety of seasonal fruits. In addition to the assortment of luscious fruits, it offers something for everyone, including exciting fall festivities such as a corn maze and horse-drawn hayrides, scrumptious doughnuts and baked goods, drool-worthy apple cider, gourmet nuts and popcorn, a lunchroom, a tasting room featuring a large variety of different flavored wines and hard ciders, along with an abutting gift shop and even a few ghosts!

The farm wasn't always owned by the Robinette family. In fact, Harvey Braman established it in 1870 with the intent to turn it into a peach farm. Due to clay loam, sandy loam soil and white oak and hickory trees being abundant on the property, it created the perfect environment to grow some of the largest and juiciest peaches in all of Michigan. Over the years, Harvey began to build up the property, erecting a red barn in 1881. Because the quality of his fruit was so great, Harvey quickly made a name for himself in

Barzilla Robinette. *Kerrie Van Eck of Robinette's Apple Haus & Winery.*

the farming community. People came from far and wide to buy up his homegrown produce. By 1910, after forty years of success as a farmer, Harvey decided that his hardworking days at the farm were over. He looked forward to retiring and selling his property to someone who would get good use out of it, so he listed it for sale in the Grand Rapids newspaper.

Ohio farmer Barzilla Robinette came up to Michigan to visit a friend from his childhood and caught a glimpse of the advertisement listing Harvey's peach farm for sale. Believing that the farm would be a good investment, Barzilla saved up and purchased the farm in 1911. He then relocated his family—including his wife, Minnie; son Allan; and daughter, Anna—to Grand Rapids Township. One year later, Barzilla's eldest son, twenty-two-year-old Edward, who was a schoolteacher at the time, left his job to move north and help with the family business.

Barzilla worked on the farm up until his passing on June 29, 1926, at eighty years old. After Barzilla's passing, Edward took over the farm and continued his father's legacy until his children took over, and so on and so forth. The farm has continued to expand and improve under the operation of the Robinette family for six generations.

At the time the Robinettes began farming in Michigan, there were a total of twelve apple orchards in the township, but today Robinette's is the only one that remains. However, the Robinette Farm didn't incorporate its Apple Haus until 1973 and typically harvested peaches in the early days. While the owners strongly value their family legacy, they have occasionally hired people outside the family to assist them, especially during the orchard's peak season.

In the fall of 2008, when the red barn was remodeled, a decision was made to convert the lower level into a rustic-themed winery. Kare Greenup was hired in that season to work as a sales associate and server. While she enjoys her job at the farm, the last thing she ever expected to encounter there was paranormal activity.

One afternoon, during a lull in business, Kare had been working in the barn and decided to run up to the second level to grab something. Once

A 1912 photograph depicting the Robinette family bound for the Grand Rapids market with fruit in tow. Edward Robinette is seated, while his brother (Allan), sister (Anna) and mother (Minnie) stand by the wagon. The barn in the backdrop is now a gift shop and winery. *Kerrie Van Eck of Robinette's Apple Haus & Winery.*

she grabbed what she needed, she started to descend the staircase when she noticed something rather unusual. There, at the foot of the wooden stairwell in the winery, stood an elderly man in a plaid flannel shirt and bib overalls, as if he was waiting for something. Kare estimated his age to be about eighty years old. He didn't say anything and just observed as Kare began making her way down the steps. When Kare reached the bottom, she was able to get a better look at the first floor and realized that the man was no longer there. She searched the winery high and low thinking that the man was a customer in need of help, but he was nowhere to be found and no one else working that day saw him either.

Ever since Kare caught a glimpse of the man, the activity seemed to amplify. She witnessed a mirror that was affixed to the wall in the winery bearing the Robinette namesake rocking back and forth despite a lack of airflow. Another time while she was working, one of the wax bowls in the gift shop that had been lying flat on the shelf appeared to have been thrown toward the center of the floor. Lastly, when stuffed animals were being sold

At the foot of this staircase is where the apparition of an elderly man has been spotted.
Kerrie Van Eck of Robinette's Apple Haus & Winery.

in the gift shop, a stuffed monkey that had been tucked into the back of the shelf also seemed to make his way from one wall to the center of the room overnight. When Kare opened the next day, she was stunned to see the stuffed toy sitting in the middle of the floor and was puzzled as to how it got there in the first place. Interestingly enough, Kare isn't the only person at the farm to have experienced the unexplainable, but she does seem to have encountered it more than others.

Not long after Kare had her brush with the metaphysical, Beverly West, who's worked at the Robinette Farm for more than twenty years, ended up having her first experience as well. It appeared to be a day like any other, and Beverly was getting the cash register in the gift shop ready for the day while another employee neatened up stock. Both employees were taken totally off guard when a porcelain doll, which had been sitting peacefully on a shelf just moments prior, aggressively flew off and was obliterated into dust as it struck the floor. An involuntary scream escaped their lips as the women stared in horror at the spectacle, wondering what spectral being was responsible for the commotion. Could it possibly be a former family member who was particular about presentation? Staff seems to think so.

Employees estimate there to be two apparitions at the orchard and believe that both are ancestors of the Robinette family. Although they can't put their finger on who exactly is roaming the first floor of the barn, they believe it to be two individuals who care an awful lot about the property itself. Maybe one of them is Barzilla Robinette himself, just checking in to make sure everything is fine. And even if it's not him, well, technically, he is still here at the old orchard in "spirit"—and I mean that literally. I bet you didn't know that the very first hard cider ever created at the farm was named after him.

If you're looking for a new place to haunt in northern Kent County, Robinette's winery is highly recommended. Best to haunt it before it haunts you!

Ale, Apparitions, Attachments and Antiques

7 Monks Taproom and Low Bar

128 South Union Street
Traverse City, MI 49684

In 2011, co-owners Matt Cozzens and Jim Smolak decided to open the very first 7 Monks Taproom in Michigan's Cherry Capital, Traverse City, just prior to Labor Day. Starting out, everything was going swimmingly. But by November 2012, there was a tangible heaviness in the air that no one had ever experienced before, and it was getting progressively worse as time went on. Where did this sensation come from? What suddenly brought it on? These questions ran through the minds of the owners and employees for years, yet there was never any explanation. Finally, in September 2022, after some truly nightmarish events, Jim and his employee, longtime bartender and manager Laura Allore, who had worked at the taproom for more than ten years, came to a conclusion that led them both down a paranormal rabbit hole.

No one could deny that 7 Monks Taproom was becoming a smashing success, so much so that the owners had an idea to open another bar in what was, at the time, just a regular damp and dimly lit basement. The idea was to create an underground pre-Prohibition speakeasy called the Low Bar, featuring period cocktails and concoctions. This new establishment would be dark and swanky, as it would be hidden from the street, and would lack windows and a television, unlike most bars nowadays.

When Laura Allore was hired in March 2012, she spent a lot of time traveling between both floors of the building, as the basement was being used strictly for bar storage at that time. If she ever needed anything, she would simply ride the elevator down, grab what she needed and come back upstairs with no issue. When Laura was informed that the basement would be undergoing a major transformation to create a whole new establishment, she was thrilled and looked forward to seeing the completed renovations.

In November 2012, the Low Bar was almost ready to open to the public, and what a sight it was to behold. Three glistening chandeliers hung above the bar, tealight candles flickered on tabletops and brass light fixtures illuminated booths. Persian rugs, red velvet curtains, black studded furniture, velvet couches and benches and a pop of brightly colored swirled wallpaper added elegance to the space, as taxidermied animals, period photographs and antique finds adorned the walls, adding mystery. Everything was coming together perfectly, and to top it all off, liquor orders began to arrive.

A delivery driver from a local distribution company arrived one afternoon to drop off the very first liquor order at the brand-new bar. It was the middle of his workday, and he was only about halfway done with his deliveries. Seeking a place to leave the order, he descended two flights of stairs to the

The glamorous underground bar is riddled with spirits. *Brian and Bridgett Beckwith.*

bar's back entrance but realized that he was totally alone as he entered the unlit and silent environment. He called out "Hello?" into the darkened basement as he sought out an employee to leave the order with. However, all the owners and employees were working in the taproom, so no one was down there to greet him. The driver's heart began racing out of nowhere, and he felt as though someone was preying on him, so he flipped on the light switch and proceeded to set the order by the entrance. At that moment, the sign for the bathroom caught his eye, and after a busy day of making deliveries, he realized that he desperately needed to use the restroom and rushed to do his business and get out of there.

Once finished, the driver washed his hands and proceeded to unlock the bathroom door; however, he noticed that the door wasn't budging. As he put a shoulder and all his might into trying to open the door, he could feel someone on the other side pushing it back with an incredible amount of force, never allowing him to fully open the door. As the driver was pushing on his end, he could see it open just a sliver, but not enough at all to make out who or what was keeping him captive. He assumed that someone at the bar was messing around with him. As he gritted his teeth and pushed even harder, the door opened wide, nearly causing the driver to fall to the ground. Expecting to see a practical joker on the other side, he was taken aback to find that the bar was still empty. Leaving the order at the entrance, the driver took off in a flash. Unfortunately for him, this would not be his last visit to the Low Bar.

The Low Bar was officially opened in 2013, and the same driver regularly delivered orders there. Once when Laura intercepted an order from him, he told her all about his horrifying experience during his first time delivering at the bar, finishing up his story with, "I absolutely dread anytime I have to stop at the Low Bar." Although Laura felt sorry for the driver, she understood exactly what he meant because the feelings and physical symptoms he encountered in the basement were the same ones Laura felt every time she went down there since the bar was implemented.

Since the printer for 7 Monks Taproom is in the back office of the Low Bar and many items continued to be stored downstairs, even after the remodel, such as glassware, liquor, cocktail mixes and more, Laura finds herself on the lower level quite often. She's even voluntarily helped with the Low Bar's banking. However, each time she'd go downstairs, she was overcome by more and more anxiety. What started as a general feeling of being watched escalated into her hair standing straight up from fear. As time progressed, Laura began to feel someone breathing down her neck and refused to go down into the bar by herself, only doing so on the condition that others were working down there as well. Her days of entering the basement alone were over.

In the spring of 2014, an employee in charge of custodial duties for both bars abruptly quit his job without giving management an official two-week notice. Later, they discovered a handwritten note left in the office in which the employee cited his reason for leaving: "the building is evil." He went on to write that he felt so perturbed in the building that he couldn't possibly continue working there any longer. He also shared that he was witness to many unearthly happenings in the basement during his time there, unfortunately never detailing exactly what he saw. Undeniably, he was very traumatized by whatever it was. What's truly bizarre is that shortly after quitting, this man went missing for an extended time. His family, friends, former bosses and co-workers did not see or hear from him, and one of his cousins even showed up at the bar looking for him, as he was nowhere to be found.

The most common happening at the Low Bar is that things never seem to stay how and where they had been left the night prior. The general manager would come into work and discover that chairs had fallen off tables and were strewn about the room, and the same could be said for one of the photographs that hangs on the back hallway wall. No matter how well secured to the wall it appeared, it tended to jump right off, causing a lot of grief for staff members, who have the constant chore of putting it back up. The most bewildering phenomenon is when the motion sensor cameras started recording during the middle of the night, sometimes for a few minutes and other times for several hours, with nothing but a few dust particles visible on the footage. This certainly gives the impression that whatever is haunting the location could potentially be a shadow figure that roams freely in the blackness of night. Although the prospect of a dark, imposing humanoid wandering through the two-story building is innately terrifying, the sounds of the falling furniture echoing throughout the structure create mental turmoil like nothing else.

On a late night in 2018, Laura and another female employee were shutting down the 7 Monks Taproom for the evening. They were the only individuals left in the building both upstairs and down. The women were going through the process of gathering up their personal belongings, clocking out, shutting off the lights and locking the doors. While they were tending to these duties, the two women began discussing all the haunted happenings that had taken place at the Low Bar. Laura was disinclined to run downstairs and make sure the back entrance was locked but figured the faster she ran down there to check, the sooner it would be over with. So, she sprinted down the steps and back up again, expressing her discomfort to the other employee. "Ugh! I just hate going down there! It is so creepy. I very rarely, if ever, go down there alone anymore, and I am just so glad that's over with for the night. I feel so much better being in 7 Monks." The two women made their way to the back door on the main floor so that they could lock up and leave. When they got about halfway there, a loud crash could be heard across the taproom. Both ladies jumped in fright and let out a scream as they frantically searched in the dark for the light switches to turn the lights back on.

Once the lights were back on, the women made a beeline for the area of the taproom where the sound came from. They thought maybe a chair had fallen off the table, but when they ran over, everything was untouched. Nothing appeared to have fallen at all. Both women were really confused and so creeped out by the incident that they didn't waste any more time in leaving for the night.

The next day, Laura told Jim about the incident, expressing concern that activity was now taking place in the taproom, a place that had seemed safe from the paranormal until recently. They talked for a bit, recalling some of the supernatural events, as well as the strange behavior exhibited by certain people while in the building. The duo suspected that a spirit had been introduced into the building during the construction of Low Bar. Because all this strange activity seemed to start up once the antiques were brought in for decoration, they assumed that the spirit was attached to at least one of the items, if not all. They largely suspected that the old photograph that didn't seem to want to stay on the wall was partially responsible for some of the happenings. For a while, Laura and Jim simply accepted their fate, not sure how to proceed going forward.

Four years later, in 2022, when Laura and Jim were contacted about being in this book about haunted bars and pubs, they began contacting individuals at once to collect their paranormal experiences. After much thought, Jim knew just the thing to do. He reached out to the woman who decorated Low Bar, as she owned an antique shop downtown and could possibly know the backstories behind some of these antiques.

"Hi, this is Jim Smolak calling from the Low Bar; you decorated my business for me in 2013 with some antiques. I was wondering if you knew anything about the antiques you used in the bar?"

"Hello Jim. Good to hear from you. Hope everything is good with you and the crew. I'd be more than happy to try and assist you with that. Let me check and see what I can find out. Do you mind if I give you a call back?"

The antique décor is presumed to be a contributing factor for the ghostly happenings on site. *Brian and Bridgett Beckwith.*

"Of course not."

"Okay, Jim. Thank you. I'll call you in a little bit."

After searching through her documentation for about an hour, the lady appeared to have found some limited information regarding the antiques and was excited to share her findings with Jim. Picking up her phone, she eagerly dialed his number. After a few short rings, Jim answered the call anxiously.

"Hey there. Any luck with uncovering the history of the items?

"I was able to locate a couple bits of information for you," the lady said exhaling. "Alright Jim, here is what I found. I am seeing that one of the chandeliers we installed in your bar is from the early 1900s and was made in France. However, it spent most of its life in Chicago. As for the other antiques, those came from the Grand Rapids area. Unfortunately, I don't have a specific person or name tied to any of them. My apologies about that. May I ask why you are inquiring about the origin of these items all these years later? Is everything ok?"

Jim hesitated as he went on. "Well, you see…we appear to have a haunting that wasn't there before the antiques were brought in. Just recently a gal reached out about writing a book and featuring our haunted bar and we were trying to find out any information that we could to help her out with the chapter."

The woman's voice perked up with enthusiasm. "Are you serious?!"

"As a heart attack."

"Jim, this is just the craziest coincidence! You're never going to believe this, but I recently had a medium come in to cleanse the shop because my employees have been experiencing so much paranormal activity and feelings of uneasiness in the shop that it was starting to affect morale!"

After Jim shared the details of this telephone conversation with Laura, both were almost too stunned to speak. They both felt that the Low Bar's paranormal claims were validated for the first time ever. It seems that whatever soul had latched on to the bygones at the bar, it wasn't good-natured in any way, shape or form. The pair are still seeking answers as to who the lost souls are that have taken up residence in the building. To up the spooky factor, the bar serves wine from Left Foot Charley, a winery that is based on the grounds of the purportedly haunted Northern Michigan Asylum.

Think you can brave two of Michigan's haunted bars in one trip? If your answer is yes, then definitely stop by 128 South Union Street in Traverse City. You won't leave disappointed.

Absolut-ely Eerie

Holden Green Tavern

151 South Broadway Street
Cassopolis, MI 49031

As a child growing up in Mishawaka, Indiana, Steve Schroeder frequently traveled twenty-two miles north with his parents to visit Cassopolis, a small village in the southwest region of Michigan with a population of under 1,800. The village is also home to Stone Lake and Diamond Lake, two of the most beautiful and crystal-clear bodies of water in the state. Steve shared some of his fondest memories in the village and always desired one day to return and open a tavern. In due course, Steve married, and the couple relocated to Iowa for numerous years before ultimately returning to Michigan, where Steve could turn his dream into a reality at last, with the help of his wife, Schelley. But upon their arrival in Cassopolis, they learned that something was amiss.

When the Schroeders returned, they looked at Cassopolis's downtown area first, eyeing up the building at 151 South Broadway Street. Built in 1897, this site had been used as one of the first post offices in the village and, over the years, was also used as a thrift store and barbershop, among other things. The structure had the historic charm that the couple was looking for, and they thought it would be in a perfect location for locals to gather, socialize and enjoy a few drinks. The Schroeders purchased the building in September 2018 from Dr. Roger Pecina, the founder of Afdent dental clinics, who had been using it as a place to store his personal collectibles and antiques. Many of those antiques, including a forty-foot-long bar from the

View of commercial buildings and automobiles along Broadway Street in Cassopolis, Michigan, date unknown. *Burton Historical Collection, Detroit Public Library.*

1930s, would find their permanent home in the Schroeders' tavern, which they named Holden Green Tavern.

For several years, the Schroeders got acquainted with the village's residents as they remodeled and repaired the old building to suit the needs of the business. During the time it took to create their ideal tavern, they learned of misfortunes in Cassopolis that seemed to vanish from people's memories like the wind whenever they were brought up. At the time of the village's inception, it was marred with horrific tragedies; at times, it almost felt as if the village itself were a magnet for these dismal occurrences.

By about 1830, many slaves had begun fleeing to what is now known as Cass County as they sought asylum in Canada, as this area of the state was one of the last stops on the Underground Railroad. More than 1,500 enslaved people made the trek, and their stories were full of triumph and tragedy. If not for the Underground Railroad Society of Cass County, this history could have potentially been forgotten forever.

The county and village were named after Lewis Cass, a former U.S. brigadier general, Michigan senator, 1848 presidential nominee and Michigan territorial governor who was widely honored around the state, despite his nefarious deeds and mastery of subterfuge. Lewis worked with President Andrew Jackson on a philanthropic plan for the Indian Removal Act, which appeared to be designed to assist the Native Americans with being mainstreamed into society. However, the executive body behind the plan believed that the Native Americans were inferior "savages" who wouldn't fit into white culture and did not have the natives' best interests at heart. Cass and his cronies ended up tricking the Native Americans into leaving by coercing them to sign treaties that would result in them losing

Lewis Cass, photographed between 1855 and 1865. *Brady-Handy Photograph Collection, Library of Congress.*

their land under the guise of helping them. This would lead to more conflicts.

According to folklore, all the misery and bitterness that Cass and his counterparts caused the natives left an imprint of negative residual energy on the area.

Cass County saw nineteen deaths in 1966 alone, making it one of the worst years in the county's history. A series of plane crashes during the year led to at least nine of those fatalities. Six individuals from Indiana were headed from Charlevoix to South Bend on a private plane when their plane suddenly fell from the sky and crashed into a wooded area just two miles from the city of Dowagiac. For six days, the plane lay in ruins until a deer hunter by the name of Glenn Ashby discovered the wreckage and promptly alerted the authorities. The victims included Mr. and Mrs. Ray Smith of Osceola, Mrs. Roy Nye of Warsaw and Mrs. Raymond Overmeyer and Mrs. Erma Vories of Mishawaka.

Just over a month later, on November 22, a similar tragedy took place when two deer hunters, Bryce Fosdick and John Vylonis of Dowagiac, lost their lives while flying over the countryside in a single-engine plane that also dropped out of the sky.

That December, the third aircraft accident of that year took place when Orville Brown, a businessman from Benton Township, decided that he wanted to take his homemade gyrocopter out for a spin. After reaching an altitude of about 1,500 feet, he plummeted to the ground below after the rotor blade on the aircraft disintegrated. The debris from the accident and Orville's body landed in proximity to the Dowagiac airport—not exactly the kind of sight you want to see if you're about to board a plane!

In addition to aircraft malfunctions that year, drownings, murders and freak accidents were also relatively commonplace. As the years went on, it appeared that this string of bad fortune continued in the area, with Cassopolis's lakes claiming many lives. All this distressed energy seemed to find its way back to Holden Green Tavern, especially when the Schroeders put out an old antique French clock dating back to the Revolutionary War.

In the summer of 2021, the multiroom tavern was opened to the public at last. Villagers couldn't wait to check it out. But as the days came and went, an unsuspecting guest began making her presence known. Villagers began reporting the sight of a middle-aged woman standing in the corner of the bar wearing clothing from an earlier time. Even though Steve and Schelley never experienced seeing the apparition in person, so many people mentioned it that they began to believe there was merit to the claims. The claims were fully validated for the Schroeders when Steve captured the figure of a woman standing in the back section of the bar on his security cameras. This happened on multiple occasions, and each time he went back there to check it out, no one was there. After the staff left for the night, the camera often picked up even more disturbances, such as an unseen force hurling shot glasses from the bar and doors slamming throughout the vacant tavern.

Another phenomenon that initially was of concern to Steve happened early in the morning when he was alone in the building and was performing opening duties down in the basement. He could hear someone tramping through the first floor as their heavy shoes struck the wooden floorboards. Knowing that the front door was locked and rushing up to see who was there, he was once again met with the sight of an empty bar. Although running a haunted business warrants uncomfortable moments, Steve remains content. "I don't feel threatened, and other than the glasses flying off the shelf, the spirit seems to be harmless. They just want to be noticed from time to time."

Steve was given further insight into who the spirit might be when a customer who identified as a psychic reader stopped in for a drink. As the woman enjoyed her cocktail, her eyes were drawn to the antique clock. Steve couldn't help but notice that she seemed spellbound by it. As she got up to examine the relic, she felt compelled to share her feelings with Steve.

"You've been dealing with an array of paranormal activity in your establishment, haven't you? I am sensing a strong female presence." Steve looked at her curiously, his claims being justified by her words. He was riveted by what she had to say next.

She continued, "I believe that this spirit has ties in some way to this antique clock that you have here. I am getting an overwhelming sensation that this woman struggled with great hardship in her life. She may have possibly been employed by a wealthy family who had this clock in their home. Could it be that she worked as their maid? I just get the sense that nothing in life was easy for her. I sense a great tragedy. She truly means you no ill will, but she doesn't want to be forgotten about. I just wanted you to know that."

Flabbergasted by the accuracy of this psychic reading, Steve recalled all the unusual happenings at his bar that had been experienced by so many in his relatively short duration as owner.

Is it possible that this spectral being could be trapped in time from the Revolutionary War? Was she possibly enslaved and desperately sought her freedom? Could she be connected in some way to one of the victims of the 1966 plane crashes? Or is she linked to some other tragedy in the Cassopolis area? And more importantly, why has this spirit decided to show itself now? The truth may forever remain concealed. Luckily, the spirit is right at home with the Schroeders.

If you're feeling courageous, the village of Cassopolis awaits your sojourn. Stop along at the two lakes to see where many met their watery ends. See if the strange energy of the village envelopes your senses. And last, but not least, come experience the haunted clock at Holden Green Tavern. There's no telling what will happen!

SPECTERS OF THE SOO

THE PALACE RESTAURANT & SALOON

200 WEST PORTAGE AVENUE
SAULT STE. MARIE, MI 49783

Sault Ste. Marie, also known as the Soo, is the oldest city in the state of Michigan, having been settled in 1668. It also shares the distinction as Michigan's most haunted city. For centuries, the dead have run rampant throughout the city's oldest locales, creating discontentment for everyone involved. Therefore, it should come as no surprise that one of the historic bars in the Soo has some seriously chilling accounts of paranormal activity revolving around its late founder.

In 1903, Finnish-born Samuel ("Sam") Viktor Kokko (formerly Karjanmaa), a Negaunee miner, who also worked at lumber camps in Newberry, saw a need for lodging in the Soo. With his vision in mind, he purchased an old paint store for $2,750 and converted it into a spectacular three-story, seventeen-room hotel and bar with ubiquitous Victorian glamour. Seeking the finest local materials for the interior, he principally used the Brunswick Company, which built the ornate, historic bar, which was brought in by railroad and installed inside the hotel. Sam also had limestone transported by barge from Drummond Island to use for the exterior of the establishment. He originally called it The Twin City Hotel. In the summer of 1907, Sam went prospecting in Cobalt, Ontario, leased out the hotel and left it under the care and direction of multiple managers associated with the family for several months. Mining during the summertime became a yearly tradition for Sam.

An antique photograph depicting when Sault Ste. Marie had dirt roads. The Twin City Hotel is pictured on the right. This photo was taken in the early 1900s. *Rob Kokko.*

Left: Samuel ("Sam") Viktor Kokko (formerly Karjanmaa). *Rob Kokko.*

Right: Elisabet ("Liisa") Kokko, née Pollari. *Rob Kokko.*

Opposite: Sam Kokko's miner's license from 1906. *Rob Kokko.*

The main level contained the bar, while the upper floors contained separate units along with a communal bathroom on each floor. Some individuals even lived at the hotel, with many of the tenants being employees of the Soo Locks, which has been a functional and iconic symbol of Sault Ste. Marie since the mid-1800s.

The Locks allow vessels to pass through Lake Superior and Lake Huron by evening out the height difference of the two lakes. In the past, without the Locks, people had to traverse the twenty-one-foot height difference by going down rapids. Since the founding of the Locks, there has been an ongoing increase in tourism, with upward of 500,000 visitors annually in recent years. While an influx of people to an area is amazing for business, it tends to be a recipe for disaster when it comes to crime.

With more people occupying the hotel and readily available liquor on location, altercations were bound to happen. Unfortunately, one of those

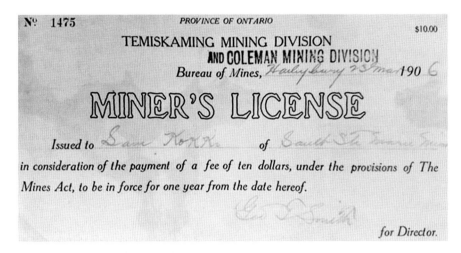

No 1475   *PROVINCE OF ONTARIO* $10.00

TEMISKAMING MINING DIVISION
AND COLEMAN MINING DIVISION
Bureau of Mines, *Haileybury 23 ma* 190 6

MINER'S LICENSE

Issued to *Sam Koxx* of *Sault Ste. Marie Sm*

in consideration of the payment of a fee of ten dollars, under the provisions of The
Mines Act, to be in force for one year from the date hereof.

for Director.

altercations resulted in a shooting, which occurred in one of the upper-floor apartments during the early 1900s while Sam was away mining. No arrest record was found regarding this shooting, so it is likely that no justice was served for the hapless victim. Sam must have had an inkling that something wasn't right because as soon as he returned to Sault Ste. Marie in the fall of 1911, he once again took back management of the hotel.

At this time, the name of the hotel was changed to the Northwest Hotel under speculation that it would deflect from the gravity of the shooting. Sam ran the hotel for ten years until he passed away on December 28, 1913, at a family wedding in Sault Ste. Marie after suffering a massive heart attack on the dance floor. He was only forty-four at the time of his passing. He left behind his wife, Elisabet ("Liisa"), another Finn whom he met while he was working in Newberry, and their eight children, consisting of five sons and three daughters (one of whom had been adopted from another family member). However, the family were prepared to take on this responsibility, as Liisa had been working alongside him until the children reached maturity. For three years after Sam's death, different business partners maintained the property until one of Sam's sons, who shared his father's first name, took over as the bar manager, while Liisa oversaw hotel operations.

As Prohibition appeared on the horizon, Sam converted the bar into a billiard hall, installing four pool tables and displaying his horde of hockey memorabilia. He also made the decision to change the name of the establishment to the Brunswick Hotel in honor of the building's magnificent original bar, which had been installed in 1903. The popularity of the business began to grow, and it became regularly patronized by professional hockey players and even the infamous Al Capone, who without question knew where to find Michigan's strongest spirits and reveled in his notoriety after creating a good deal of his own.

Sadly, tragedy struck the Kokko family again during the Great Depression. Sixty-three-year-old Liisa was spending time at the eighty-acre farm in Dafter, now Brimley Township, that she and her late husband had owned. It was a side business where they farmed hay for other farmers and raised wild turkeys. On May 18, 1935, a toilworn Liisa started pouring what she believed was fuel oil into the boiler without realizing that it was actually gasoline. Before she realized her error, the stove erupted in a powerful explosion, which seared her entire body, leaving her covered in grotesque burns and whimpering in excruciating pain. The injuries she sustained would end up claiming her life that same day. The Kokko family somehow found the strength to carry on for a number of years without her, although their lives would never be the same again.

After seventy years of ownership, the Kokko family made the tough decision to sell their cherished hotel to Delmar and Diane Newman. The name of the business was changed for the last time to The Palace Saloon, and the owners examined various ways to evolve. A new kitchen was installed so that the Newmans could begin offering Mexican cuisine along with alcoholic beverages. A few short years later, in 1977, William Kammers became the proud owner of The Palace Saloon. Just two years after he purchased the building, an uncontrollable fire ripped through the upper floors. Regardless of this inferno, restoration was prompt, and the business was able to reopen that same year. The fourth owner, Bonnie Krempel, purchased the property in 1981 and ran the business for eighteen years, further expanding the customer base. When Bonnie retired in 1999, Robert and Doreen Goetz bought out the property, and Tammy Goetz Cook became the present-day owner and operator.

Since the Goetzes have taken over, the interior and exterior of the property have undergone renovations, but one thing remains the same at this twentieth-century hostelry: the dead never sleep.

Although Tammy has never had a paranormal experience, many current and previous employees have. There have been dozens of reports of unusual happenings in almost every room, with the bar seeming to witness the bulk of the activity.

The apparition of an elder Sam Kokko has been spotted alongside two different ladies at table no. 6, which is the bar's corner booth. This booth was always Sam's favorite place to sit while he was still alive. Workers realized that they weren't dealing with living, breathing human beings because Sam and the ladies were wearing Victorian apparel, looked ghastly in appearance and dematerialized as soon as they were acknowledged. Presumably one of the ladies is Liisa, while the other is a former hotel employee. Even though these figures shy away from attention, they are quite mischievous.

After multiple episodes of finding broken glass in front of the bar, staff decided to move the glasses to a safer location. On a breezy August evening, after the annual Michigan Paranormal Convention concluded for the day, a medium came with some friends to The Palace Saloon for dinner. The group sat at table no. 6, which began stirring up some visions for the seasoned reader. When the waiter approached the table to take their order, a large smile spread across the spiritualist's face. "Thank goodness you don't have to worry about those darn glasses breaking anymore, eh?"

The waiter stared dumbstruck at the woman, hesitant to respond. Another attentive employee came up from behind the waiter and said, "Sorry, I overheard you mention your awareness about us recently having to move our glasses. We had to keep replacing them, and it became absolutely maddening. How did you hear about it?"

The medium chuckled a little bit. "They told me," she said pointing her two index fingers up at the ceiling. "The spirits are laughing at you guys for doing all that work. It's just so comical to them. I apologize for giggling about it. I can just see them cracking up together. They're so bad. I sincerely hope it wasn't too taxing."

As the two workers quickly glanced around at the bar filled with convention goers decked out in Bigfoot and ghost graphic tees, they caught on that they were in the presence of a medium. "Well, I'm glad they enjoyed the view," the employee said, laughing as she turned to walk away, snapping her order notepad shut.

That same night, while one of the bartenders was closing up, she could hear people moving about in the building not long after she had locked the doors. It frightened her so much that she made a phone call to the police to come out and investigate. When the police arrived, the bartender stepped outside to wait for the verdict. The police officers returned from their inspection, failing to produce any evidence. An electrician had a very similar experience when he was commissioned for an overnight job at The Palace Saloon. He had shut off the electricity as he worked and could hear what sounded like someone trudging through the bar. Shortly thereafter, the electrician headed home, totally scared stiff by the encounter.

Strange sounds and sightings are just a fraction of what people experience at the bar. Other reports include staff being touched on both shoulders as

This historic hotel/bar is considered one of the most haunted places in the Soo. *Michelle Jean Blankenship.*

if someone was standing behind them and their shoulders being brushed by what felt like a phantom body passing them as they made their way to the second floor.

After all sorts of electrical disturbances took place throughout the entire building, the maintenance man was making his rounds and discovered that all the lightbulbs in the basement had been unscrewed, even though they were covered and secured by metal cages. This began to happen frequently and became so annoying for the maintenance man and staff alike that he ultimately decided to remove the cages once and for all.

Hopefully you will find your way to Michigan's most haunted city, as it is chock full of both beauty and mystery. Maybe you'll even plan your vacation to the Soo at the end of August so you can attend the Michigan Paranormal Convention. Then you can pick the brains of those who investigate and speak with the dead and afterward enjoy a bite to eat at a real haunted location. Who knows, you may even cross paths with the soul of Sam Kokko while you're here. If you're feeling afraid, just remember that The Palace Saloon serves more than 120 different types of tequila from all over the world, so drinking your way to bravery will not be a problem.

WALTER THE WANDERER

THIRSTY LLAMA PUB N GRUB

5990 WEST MAIN STREET
WEIDMAN, MI 48893

If you've made it this far in the book, then you should already know by now that spirits don't seem to have any regard for personal boundaries. They've snuck up on people at the most unexpected and vulnerable of times and will likely continue to do so as long as there are people on planet Earth. We've already established that usually spirits seem to have a connection of some sort to the location itself or the owners, but every situation is unique. Just like in life, some spirits can find themselves lost, continually searching for the place where they belong, as seems to be the case in this story. After scouring historical records for months, it doesn't appear that a man named Walter ever worked at 5990 West Main Street, a building that is supposedly one of the oldest in all of Weidman. However, the wandering apparition that answers to the name somehow found his way to this address and has been quite the trickster there ever since.

It's no revelation that there are a few wayfaring spirits in this neck of the woods, especially considering Central Michigan's checkered history. Isabella County, located smack dab in the middle of mid-Michigan, originally had a bountiful supply of lush forestlands. For about ten thousand years, the Saginaw Chippewa American Indian Tribe used this land for hunting and gathering before European settlers arrived. They called it *Ojibway Besse*, which translates to "the place of the Chippewa." This arable land currently houses the Isabella Indian Reservation and myriad farms.

The structure that currently houses the pub started as the first livery stable in the small town of Weidman and was located just east of the corner hotel. A businessman by the name of Bob Aylsworth was running a saloon out of the hotel until May 15, 1901, when an unprecedented fire swept through the area, destroying nearly the entire Burdick block and causing more than $12,000 in damages, which is the equivalent of just over $42,000 in today's dollars. To make matters worse, the businesses that burned were only partially insured. Wasting no time in trying to recover his losses, Bob relocated his saloon into the surviving stable. He called it The Quail Tavern and Pool Room, and it was managed by Bob's friend Charles Johnson. From that day forward, the building was primarily used as a drinking establishment, although it did contain a cigar shop early on.

Portrait of a Native American man of the Saginaw Chippewa American Indian Tribe. Photo copyrighted in 1903 by Salling, Hanson & Company. *Library of Congress.*

Fred Bartlett was the second owner, turning the business into Bartlett's Café. The place was then sold again at the onset of the Great Depression to Charlie and Agnes Gross. Obviously, the Grosses felt undefeated by this dispiriting time in history and delighted in their new undertaking, which they aptly renamed The Weidman Café.

On June 19, 1941, another fire wreaked havoc on five businesses in Weidman, badly damaging the dated structure. The Grosses restored and remodeled the building. They added additional rooms for storage and dancing, as well as an updated kitchen. They also utilized a team of horses to dig out a basement. These changes ensured the success of the business for decades as it provided a bit of nightlife. As might be expected, more owners came and went through the years, and the business adopted new names, a few being The Idle Hour and The Side Street Café. Meanwhile, other bars and restaurants began popping up in Isabella County, and it seemed that patronage came to a standstill. For more than twenty years, the building stood as a shell of its former self until 2019, when Terry Bonnau and Jay

Burnett acquired the property and breathed new life into the place, calling it the Thirsty Llama Pub N Grub.

The years had not been kind to this weathered brick erection, and upon setting foot through its doors, Terry and Jay knew they had a fixer-upper on their hands. They hadn't a clue that Walter was waiting in the wings for them. The two men grabbed their toolboxes and got to work tout de suite. But during times when they were working alone, their tools would keep coming up missing.

Terry found himself in an anomalous situation when, while in the process of handyman work, he set a hammer or drill down and then went to pick it back up again only to realize that the tool was gone. Later, in the day, when Terry would return to the area where he lost his tool, the missing item would be lying right where he left it in the first place, as if it had been sitting there the whole time. Terry had immediate suspicions that the old building was haunted, but as a Native American he embraced the nomadic soul, regardless of his irksome qualities.

After completing some necessary updates on the building, the men brought in a few unique furnishings to give their place some character. One of those pieces included a monk's chair from South America. With almost everything ready to go, Terry and Jay couldn't wait to welcome customers into the Thirsty Llama.

Just days before opening, a meeting took place at the pub. Terry—along with his food representative, pub manager and head cook—was discussing logistics when a thunderous *clang* resounded throughout the building that sounded like toppling cookware. Everyone was rattled by the racket. As the food representative stood up to leave, he smirked, "Well fellas, it seems you have a ghost! I better get going so you can check out whatever that was," he said, motioning his hand toward the kitchen. He then thanked each person for their time as he said goodbye and proceeded to wave upward in the direction of the kitchen ceiling, facetiously bidding the ghost farewell. After the food representative left, Terry and the two other gentlemen he had with him could not see a single pot or a pan out of place. This was the day Walter formally announced, "Hey everyone! I'm here!"

During one of his first late-night shifts, Terry began mingling with one of the female customers at the bar. They were discussing all sorts of things from the weather to how the bar came to be when the woman instantaneously stopped paying attention to what Terry was saying as she felt someone begin stroking her hair. She urgently reached up to grasp the hair at the base of her skull.

"You all right?" Terry asked, concerned. The woman looked up at him goggle-eyed, letting out a gasp of horror as a piece of her hair on the right side that had been draped down her back proceeded to lift slowly off her shoulder, higher and higher into the air until it was almost standing straight up. A moment later, another piece of hair on her left side that was also down her back was placed in front of her shoulder. Terry watched in bewilderment as this happened right in front of his nose. The woman continued to sit aghast as the intangible spirit rearranged her auburn tresses.

This certainly was not the first woman Walter has put his hands on and won't be the last. He is one of those spirits that lacks the understanding of personal boundaries. The man obviously thinks he has serious game in the afterlife, but instead he just has the audacity. There is certainly no denying that Walter's funny business is in full swing, especially when it comes to pretty women. But Terry had no way of knowing that Walter was just getting his feet wet and that the tomfoolery that didn't involve flirting with the living would wind up costing Terry and Jay money.

One of the newly hired bartenders was taking a rest in the monk's chair when she heard the high-pitched clatter of glass hit the floor. Rushing into the kitchen, she spied one of the globe lighting fixtures that had been protecting a bulb on the kitchen ceiling had snapped into several chunks upon impact with the floor. Every subsequent shift she had after that, one of the globes would either fall or move, almost in protest of her sitting on the chair. This even happened in the wee hours of the morning when the pub had no customers. At daybreak, when Terry arrived at work, he could see that three of the lighting globes had been placed on a cutting board that was on the countertop. Each globe was stacked very neatly, one on top of the other. All the activity up until this point had been a bit bothersome but far from pestilent.

It was a no-brainer that Walter craved even more attention, so he threw caution to the wind in the hopes of making an impact. This time around, he began creating big messes. The first noteworthy event took place when Terry was working with the bartender and there was a limited number of customers in the bar. He was standing just over six feet away from the reach-in cooler, which was located next to the door of the dining room. The bartender came up behind him, and thinking she was going into the dining room he stepped aside, moving in front of the tap cooler. Instead, she went to the reach-in cooler, and when she opened the door to grab a beer for one of the customers, one of the bottles that was in the back of the cooler behind the divider went airborne. Instead of falling to the floor below, it hurtled

Making messes is Walter's forte. *Monica Chambers of Thirsty Llama Pub N Grub.*

toward Terry, splitting open on the edge of the tap cooler. The customer, who was nearby, surely had something to write home about that day!

The second event consisted of, once again, coming into work early to find the walk-in cooler in complete disarray. Two cases of beer were lying sideways on the floor, with many of the bottles broken, and a sticky pool of lager surrounding them. One of the bags of lettuce that was stored on the opposite wall with other vegetables and meats was lying near the mess. How this leafy veggie teleported from one side of the room-sized cooler to the other is quite an enigma.

Walter the Wanderer may not have to wander much longer, since he is welcome to stay at the pub, but he's going to have to learn how to behave himself. He takes advantage of his invisibleness much like we all would if given an opportunity. He gets a kick out of raiding the refrigerated pantry, being playful and keeping staff on their toes. However, the one thing Walter enjoys most of all is meeting new female customers. Walter may hang around the bar, but the only thing he is thirsty for is the company of a single babe. When visiting, be on your guard, ladies!

Sláinte Among the Spooks

Coonan's Irish Hub

1004 North Johnson Street
Bay City, MI 48708

Across cities around the world, there are a few food and drink establishments that seem to soar above the rest. They are places that most of the city's population has visited, and if for whatever reason a few stragglers haven't been, they at least are familiar with the name. For Bay City, that place is Coonan's Irish Hub. Despite being built in 1955, the pub has made quite a name for itself and has even garnered higher approval ratings among the locals than some of the older bars in the area. The pub is highly regarded for its homemade Irish fare, with one of the best dishes on the menu being the Guinness stew. But you'd likely be surprised to learn that Coonan's Irish Hub has a resident ghost. And oddly enough, he isn't Irish at all!

Walter ("Wattie") Mullins, a West Virginian of English and French descent, put down roots in Bay City and decided to open his own tavern in the Johnson Street Business District across from where Coonan's Irish Hub stands today.

After working for several years, he decided that he wanted to expand the size of his tavern and had his sights set on available land across the street where he could build a larger pub. In 1960, the Hub Bar opened to the public and, without delay, became a meeting place for those looking to make friends and greet their neighbors.

As the years crept by, the once robust Mr. Mullins became a frail little old man. Customers didn't fail to notice that he appeared to have lost inches in stature and a road map of wrinkles now covered his haggard face. They trailed from the veiny lids of his deep-set eyes to his reddened nose to his cyanotic lips. His face told a story of a man who knew a life of nothing but hard work. Incessantly shivering from poor circulation and the piercing Michigan wind in the winter months, Wattie was always seen bundled up in his signature woolen button-down sweater with a flat cap on his noggin. Salt-and-pepper facial hair decorated his face. His decrepit appearance never drove away newcomers since he never left the house without a charming smile or an air of benignity. Wattie was slowing down, and it was a hard pill to swallow for many who grew close to him.

When Bruce Wolff became the pub's new owner in 1966, it seemed that Wattie Mullins faded away from the bar scene and that his legacy was on its way to becoming a distant memory. The circumstances of what transpired in his final moments at Mercy Hospital on May 23, 1973, at age seventy, are not widely known. He would eventually be seen again, although not in the flesh.

Louis and Sharon Arnold purchased the property on March 20, 1975, and changed the name to The Hub. It then took a total of thirty-six additional years before the spirit of Mr. Mullins was awakened. As the story goes, the old-timer had taken up an eternal residence at the pub and had been dormant until an Irish American man by the name of Kim Coonan purchased the pub. Soon after, spiritually gifted members of his family and the community drew out Wattie from his slumber.

Kim, a former union organizer, had retired at a young age and was looking for something productive to do with his time. After reminiscing about all the happy memories he shared as a child at his grandfather's bar, Revette's, he decided to try his own hand at bar ownership. On May 31, 2011, Kim took over as proprietor. Staying true to the bar's provenance and paying homage to his Irish heritage, he renamed the bar Coonan's Irish Hub. From the very beginning, Kim's whole family, including his two daughters, Sheryl and Erin, and his grandchildren, wholeheartedly supported his new enterprise.

In the summer of that same year, Erin Coonan-Whisman began working as the pub's part-time manager since she was also working full time as a cosmetologist and a doting mother of three. Fully immersed in her first shift as manager one day, she barely noticed that a radio had turned on in the building. Not thinking much of it, she turned it off and went about the rest of her day. This proceeded to happen day after day, with Erin having to

Kim Coonan hard at work. *Erin Coonan-Whisman of Coonan's Irish Hub.*

shut off the radio sometimes four times in a single shift. Assuming that the radio was broken, they got rid of it and over time had several different sound systems installed by professionals, but the systems continued to turn on when no one was near the controls. Early on, the Coonans also had a coin-operated jukebox inside the pub. On an especially slow night, Erin decided to head out early. She went outside to lock the door, and just as she turned the key, she could hear Billy Joel's song "Piano Man" playing loudly as colors of the rainbow emanated from the jukebox, glimmering throughout the darkened space. Erin found the song choice uncanny, considering it painted the picture of a typical bar scene with undertones of loneliness and despair. After some time, the Coonans did away with the jukebox.

After six years of sleepless nights juggling two demanding jobs and caring for her family, Erin decided to quit her full-time gig to dedicate more time and attention to the pub. This decision afforded Erin the opportunity to help with the onboarding of new hires and get to know them on a one-on-one basis.

Trisha Pergande, an employee of Coonan's for more than four years, was working in the storage room one day when she felt eyes on her. She kept glancing over her right shoulder to make sure that she was still alone in the room. The final time she glanced back, she saw a spectral visitor behind her. Trisha's description of the spirit was identical to what Wattie Mullins looked like later in his life. The soul looked to be a septuagenarian and was garbed in a woolen sweater and cap. Instead of feeling afraid, Trisha was surprised by the overwhelming joy and happiness she felt. Worried about being judged, she only confided in Erin by simply saying that she saw a spirit but unfortunately spared her the details. Erin then revealed that she also had paranormal encounters at the pub and shared in-depth stories about what happened with the radio and jukebox during her first few years as manager. At the close of their conversation, she told Trisha that she considered herself to be an intuitive medium. Since that day, Trisha has had recurring run-ins with Wattie and finds his presence to be a great comfort, feeling that his only intention is to make sure that the pub stays in good hands.

A few weeks after Trisha had her first experience, Erin and another female employee (who has chosen to remain anonymous) were filling condiments in the storage room when suddenly a shadowy older man came into Erin's peripheral vision. He stood at her right side for several seconds before morphing into a small shape and zooming over both ladies' heads, disappearing into the walk-in cooler at full tilt. "Oh my God! Did you just see that?!" Erin inquired, bolting upright as she felt a surge of adrenaline rip through her veins.

The other employee, visibly afraid, uncomfortably shifted her gaze toward the floor. "Well, yes, but if I don't acknowledge it, then it won't bother me." With this employee adamantly refusing to discuss what just occurred, Erin went to find Trisha so she could find out if they saw the same figure.

As Erin began describing the apparition, Trisha turned to her calmly and said, "You mean you saw the elfin-looking man in the back with the hat?"

"What?! Are you serious?! That's the same person you saw?" Erin asked.

"Mmhmm, that's him alright," Trisha affirmed. "I see him all the time now around here."

This information bonded Erin and Trisha that day, as the two discovered that they shared the gift of spiritual sensitivity. Rachael Schulz, a regular of Coonan's, would soon catch sight of Wattie as well, much to her astonishment.

About eight years ago, Rachael's wife brought her to Coonan's so that she could try the famous stew and some of the beers on tap. Stepping into the bar for the first time, Rachael felt as though she had stepped into the past, to a simpler era, where the latest and greatest technology didn't matter, and only human interactions did. Through Rachael's patronage, she became good friends with the Coonan family. As often as possible, Rachael and her wife make the half-hour trip from Sebewaing to Bay City to spend time at their favorite pub. One evening, the women arrived just in time to have one drink before the establishment closed. Erin had been working that night, and the three ladies were sitting around mingling when they all heard something dragging across the floor in the other room. When the ladies showed concern, Erin assured them that everything was alright and that staff have been encountering paranormal activity at the pub regularly. Rachael told Erin that she most certainly believed her because she was picking up on some residual energy in the building.

Just as those words left her mouth, she looked up at the mirror behind the bar and could see a black mist forming into a humanoid shape. An older man looked back at her, and she studied the wrinkles at the corner of his eyes and took note of the gray flecks that were scattered throughout his facial hair. Fearful of what she was seeing, Rachael leaped back in fright, but after calming her nerves she got the sense that this man was a gentle soul, later describing him as having "an aura of love."

Erin was thrilled that yet another person saw the same spirit that she and Trisha saw, further validating that Wattie is where he truly belongs. Wattie is in good company, as a few of the Coonan ancestors have also adopted Coonan's as their home in the afterlife, with one of the spirits being Erin's Uncle Billy.

Billy was Kim's older brother who was born cognitively challenged. During the last several years of his life, Kim took care of him and even shared his home with him. Billy was a car aficionado, and to boost his mood, Kim would take him out to learn how to drive. Billy was enraptured by these experiences, beaming from ear to ear as he and his younger brother navigated new terrain. He loved cars so much that he carried an assortment of keys with him that he collected from different family members and loved showing them off to everyone he met.

After getting approval from her father, Erin removed Sundays from Coonan's days of operation so that they could have time for the family to get together. Occasionally, they would use that time to tend to chores at the bar, as they had the entire unattended space to themselves. One Sunday, Erin was at the bar with her son and father, as well as her boyfriend, Todd, and his daughter. While the place wasn't open to the public, Kim had his keys locked inside the front door. After three hours had passed, an awestruck Todd, who was about ten feet away from the door, exclaimed loudly, "Look at the keys!"

Everyone stared at the door in incredulity as the keys vigorously swung back and forth in the keyhole by themselves for twenty seconds before stopping. With a tear in her eye, Erin conceded that Uncle Billy was letting everyone know that he was okay on the other side.

From time to time, Grandma Coonan has passed through the pub as well—the only trace being the scent of her floral perfume lingering in the air and captivating the ones who loved her more than life itself.

Rather than live in fear of these mystical beings that populate the pub, Erin thinks of them as a blessing instead. "I feel honored that the spirits choose to spend time with us at our bar, along with all the fantastic people who come in. We are on this earth together for just the blink of an eye, and I am going to try and enjoy every second of it." If you're a Hibernophile who has no reservations about raising a glass and shouting "*Slainte!*" among the spooks, you'll absolutely love Coonan's Irish Hub.

BIBLIOGRAPHY

Acosta, Roberto. "Fire Damages Apartment, Museum in Downtown Davison." MLive, August 31, 2015. https://www.mlive.com/news/flint/2015/08/fire_damages_apartment_museum.html#incart_river.

Albert, Samantha. "The Underground Railroad Society of Cass County Is Educating the Community on Its Almost Lost History." WNDU, February 7, 2022. https://www.wndu.com/2022/02/07/underground-railroad-society-cass-county-is-educating-community-its-almost-lost-history.

Albuquerque Morning Journal. "Albuquerque Boy Dies in Detroit." April 15, 1911.

Allen Funeral Home Inc. https://www.allenfuneralhomeinc.com.

Ashley, Skyler. "Investigating Campus Hauntings with the MSU Paranormal Society." City Pulse, August 4, 2018. https://www.lansingcitypulse.com/stories/investigating-campus-hauntings-with-the-msu-paranormal-society,556.

Atlas Obscura. "The Red Lion." https://www.atlasobscura.com/places/the-red-lion.

Bauer, Patricia. "Bath School Disaster." Encyclopædia Britannica, 2020. https://www.britannica.com/event/Bath-school-disaster-1927.

Bay City Times. "Announcement: Your New Hub Bar Now Open!" April 9, 1960.

———. "Up for Transfer." September 22, 1966.

———. "W.E. Mullins." May 23, 1973.

Bay County Historical Society. Bay City Directory (1959–2008).

Beal City Centennial Committee. Beal City, Michigan, Area Centennial, 1875–1975.

Beauchamp, Nicole. *Haunted Detroit*. Charleston, SC: The History Press, 2022.

Bicsak, Sarah. "Campus Legends and Myths." On the Banks of the Red Cedar, May 2013. https://onthebanks.msu.edu/Exhibit/1-6-13/campus-legends-and-myths.

Boyles, David. "Michigan Drinking Age History." Study, December 21, 2021. https://study.com/academy/lesson/michigan-drinking-age-history.html?fbclid=IwAR14GdsXgq3AyHWqv3jGb5DRPs6Lvo7ur8cR110E8s4yslSQ7dEABqtbZsY.

Canterbury Village. "Keatington Village." 2014. https://canterburyvillage.com/index.php/about-us/23-keatington-village.

Chapman Bros. *Portrait and Biological Album of Oakland County, Michigan*. Chicago: self-published, 1891.

Congleton, Gerry. "Cities, Buildings, Named for Lewis Cass a Wrong to Native Americans that Must Be Corrected." Yahoo! News, December 5, 2021. https://www.yahoo.com/news/cities-buildings-named-lewis-cass-120115198.html.

Coonan's Irish Hub. https://coonansirishhub.com.

Culton, Sarah. "Holden Green Tavern Opens in Downtown Cassopolis." Leader Publications, August 19, 2021. https://www.leaderpub.com/2021/08/19/holden-green-tavern-opens-in-downtown-cassopolis.

Cultural Economic Development Task Force. "Jamesport Brewing Company." Mason County Culture, October 15, 2018. http://masoncountyculture.com/business/jamesport-brewing-company.

Cultural Landscape Foundation. "William E. Scripps Estate." October 16, 2009. https://www.tclf.org/landslides/william-e-scripps-estate.

Daily Herald. "Destroyed One Block." May 17, 1901.

DesOrmeau, Taylor. "The Average Michigander Drinks 23 Gallons of Alcohol Per Year—Here's the Breakdown by Beer, Wine, Liquor." MLive, February 16, 2022. https://www.mlive.com/public-interest/2022/02/the-average-michigander-drinks-23-gallons-of-alcohol-per-year-heres-the-breakdown-by-beer-wine-liquor.html#:~:text=The%20average%20Michigander%20drinks%2023%20gallons%20of%20alcohol.

Detroit Free Press. "Five Weidman Stores Burn; Loss $30,000." June 20, 1941.

———. "Personals." June 14, 1922.

Detroit Historical Society. "William E. Scripps Mansion." 2022. https://detroithistorical.org/shop/tickets/william-e-scripps-mansion.

Dexter Area Fire Department. "History." https://dexterareafire.org/more/history.php.

Edwards, Ralph. "Emmons Butler Gill (1863–1942)." Find A Grave, November 11, 2010. https://www.findagrave.com/memorial/61454100/emmons-butler-gill.

———. "Helen Mary 'Nellie' Bush Gill (1867–1951)." Find A Grave, November 11, 2010. https://www.findagrave.com/memorial/61454069/helen-mary-gill.

Eisinger, Sara. "The Palace Restaurant and Saloon Will Come Back from COVID 'with a Swing.'" *Soo Leader*, February 10, 2022. https://www.sooleader.com/lets-eat/the-palace-restaurant-and-saloon-will-come-back-from-covid-with-a-swing-5048028?fbclid=IwAR3Co8MXv5nD2XI9o5SKfc3jBLsW31y5ycMSrOzd0VH4qpLoIiw-RNBHiFs.

Escanaba Daily Press. "Attends Meeting." September 17, 2022.

———. "Child, 3, Dies at Marquette." February 1, 1941.

———. "Council Supports City Manager at Manistique." January 13, 1970.

———. "Illness Is Fatal to Henry T. Jahn." July 19, 1958.

———. "You'll Like This Better BEER!" July 20, 1939, 18.

Evenings News. "Sault's Colorful Brunswick Hotel Under New Ownership." July 25, 1973.

Fausett Family Funeral Homes. "Obituary for Edna L. Jahn at Fausett Funeral Homes-MSTQ." March 27, 2007. https://www.fausettfh.com/obituary/651331.

Find A Grave. "Barzilla Allan Robinette (1845–1926)." October 23, 2011. https://www.findagrave.com/memorial/79166563/barzilla-allan-robinette.

———. "Marie Lakeman (1950–1995)." December 14, 2013. https://www.findagrave.com/memorial/121751060/marie-lakeman.

———. "Scio Cemetery in Dexter, Michigan." January 6, 2016. https://www.findagrave.com/cemetery/2599892/scio-cemetery.

Flint Journal. "Erwood C. 'Ray' Raysin Obituary (2015)." Via Legacy.com. August 30, 2015. https://obits.mlive.com/us/obituaries/flint/name/erwood-raysin-obituary?pid=175688877.

Fruit Growers News. "Robinette's Turns 100—Switching to Retail Helps Farm Market Last a Century." July 5, 2011. https://fruitgrowersnews.com/article/robinettes-turns-100-switching-to-retail-helps-farm-market-last-a-century.

Greco, Rachel. "Michigan Ghost Hunters to Visit Charlotte Saloon." *Battle Creek Enquirer*, April 21, 2014. https://www.battlecreekenquirer.com/story/news/2014/04/21/michigan-ghost-hunters-to-visit-charlotte-saloon/7959723.

Griffith, Mike. "Lansing Bowlers Lose a Friend." *Lansing State Journal*, February 19, 1989.

Hansen Funeral Home. "Obituary for Marion L Raysin at Hansen Funeral Home." November 14, 2016. https://www.hansenfuneralhome.net/obituary/4005904.

Haunted Britain. "The Red Lion Inn, Avebury—at Home with the Ghosts." 2020. https://www.haunted-britain.com/red-lion-inn-avebury.htm.

Herald-Palladium. "Nine Are Killed in Plane Crashes—Cass County Also Has 2 Murders, 4 Drownings." December 31, 1966.

Hoffman, Mary. "About." Marley's Bar & Grill, 2020. https://marleysvictorianpub.com/home/about.

Holst, Jan. "Robinette Family Celebrates a Century of Tending Its Orchards." MLive, March 27, 2012. https://www.mlive.com/ada-cascade/2012/03/robinette_family_celebrates_a.html.

Infinity Graphic Design/Dark Minds Productions. "A Ghost Hunters Adventure/T.R.U.E./Blue Pelican." YouTube, February 11, 2012. https://www.youtube.com/watch?v=1txtLdwWpiQ.

Isabella County Michigan. "About Isabella County." 2022. https://www.isabellacounty.org/about-isabella-county.

Jackman, Michael. "Abick's Bar Is that Corner Joint Where You Meet Your Neighbors and Share a Drink with Your Priest." *Detroit Metro Times*, October 5, 2016. https://www.metrotimes.com/detroit-guides/abicks-bar-is-that-corner-joint-where-you-meet-your-neighbors-and-share-a-drink-with-your-priest-2467366.

Jamesport Brewing Company. "JBC History." https://jamesport brewingcompany.com/history.

Kane, Jim. "Dexter Historical Groups Restoring Cemeteries." Ann Arbor District Library, via the *Ann Arbor News*, October 17, 1971. https://aadl.org/aa_news_19711017_p3-dexter_historical_group_restoring_cemeteries.

Kokko, Robert, and Lisa Kokko. "Photo of Elisabet (Liisa) Pollari Contributed by Lisa and Robert Kokko." Ancestry.com. 2022. https://www.ancestry.com/sharing/31669279?h=e94c0f&fbclid=IwAR3x7wWoEymPDndpgHLTwMsGcqjwac3QMG5yLpfWtScE7nNlK53yV8jr4i4.

———. "Photo of Samuel Viktor Kokko (Karjanmaa) Contributed by Lisa and Robert Kokko." Ancestry.com. 2022. https://www.ancestry.com/sh aring/31669162?h=28d400&fbclid=IwAR2eqlp4i7XLaOP2iPiWiy1bm IoOvL4DO5cPMA-glwBzSmKLMzw11Txkchg.

Krcek Allen, Nancy. "The Blue Pelican Inn Flies High." *Northern Express*, June 29, 2009. https://www.northernexpress.com/news/food/article-3970-the-blue-pelican-inn-flies-high/?fbclid=IwAR15gghr-P08v_3-nFsu 1yOBeqgUcrdrLVS19poU9QRKieEGR5NNNTouZ6w.

Lansing State Journal. "Listing Exchange Sales Soar to $727,995 Total." November 16, 1947.

———. "Obituaries: Nora Rashid, Business Owner." February 14, 1989.

LeDuc, M. Vonciel. *Manistique*. Charleston, SC: Arcadia Publishing, 2009.

Lyons, Mickey. "Abick's Bar, a Neighborhood Institution for More than a Century." Model D, December 31, 2014. https://www.modeldmedia. com/features/abicks-123114.aspx.

Miller, Christine. "Is the Avebury Red Lion Pub the Most Haunted Pub Ever?" Spooky Isles, October 24, 2020. https://www.spookyisles.com/ avebury-red-lion-pub.

MLive. "Fire Damages Apartment and Museum in Downtown Davison." YouTube, 2015. https://www.youtube.com/watch?v=dXmrnnAfjrc.

Orion Historical Society. "Scripps Estate." https://orionhistoricalsociety. org/scripps-estate.

Orion Neighborhood Television. "Where Living Is a Vacation: Scripps Estate." YouTube, 2022. https://www.youtube.com/watch?v=0a-eel2D0mI.

The Palace. "Our Story Started in 1903." 2023. https://www.thepalace mexicanrestaurant.com/our-story.

Pawlick, Thomas. "Review of *Your Neighbor at Work*: Variety Spices Barman's Life." *Bay City Times*, September 1, 1968.

Peterson, Larry. "Manistique's Great Fire of September 1893." Schoolcraft County Historical Society, September 6, 2016. https://schs. cityofmanistique.org/manistiques-great-fire-september-1893.

Pickleball Insider. "Robinette's Farm." July 6, 2021. https:// pickleballinsider.com/listing/robinettes-farm.

Pure Michigan. "Michigan Apples." November 23, 2016. https://www. michigan.org/michigan-apples.

Robinson, John. "Haunted Michigan: Do You Dare Lie Down in This Open Grave?" 99.1 WFMK, October 9, 2018. https://99wfmk.com/ warlocksgrave2017/?fbclid=IwAR3tLWr4f_unnbx9seqrASvujx5Ap-4XKyn1ALvxi8O2ui6kQXgpWudEcrA.

Sault Ste. Marie, Pure Michigan. "The Soo Locks, Sault Ste. Marie." 2022. https://saultstemarie.com/attractions/soo-locks/?fbclid=IwAR2zwB61-0MyOAe02g_w0xYM2yxzdFfXmj_nFk785W8_tXxaDgAxm4elAS4.

Sherman, Amy. "Greenhouses Sprouted at Dexter Beer Grotto for Outdoor Dining Crowd." MLive, February 11, 2021. https://www.mlive.com/michigansbest/2021/02/greenhouses-sprouted-at-dexter-beer-grotto-for-outdoor-dining-crowd.html.

Simpson-Mersha, Isis. "Michigan's Best Local Eats: Try the Giant Mimosa with Mini Donuts and Bacon or Giant Pizza Bloody Mary at This Davison Eatery." MLive, March 5, 2022. https://www.mlive.com/news/flint/2022/03/michigans-best-local-eats-try-the-giant-mimosa-with-mini-donuts-and-bacon-or-giant-pizza-bloody-mary-at-this-davison-eatery.html.

Soard, Lori. "Teenagers in the 1920s." LoveToKnow. https://teens.lovetoknow.com/Teenagers_in_the_1920s#:~:text=The%20invention%20of%20the%20automobile%20also%20meant%20kids.

Terry, Tanya. "Doll Museum." Davison Index, December 15, 2016. https://davisonindex.mihomepaper.com/articles/doll-museum/?fbclid=IwAR3DXOGEjYi92q3xeZRsMV-Ra0GIpB9AiV_TChGy7Hb76LcoDUjS7bWA2vI.

Times Herald. "Big Fire at Weidman." May 16, 1901.

Traverse City Record-Eagle. "Central Lake Is Found Resort Region Center." June 28, 1930.

———. "Mrs. E.B. Gill Dies." March 24, 1951.

———. "When in Central Lake Stop at the New Tavern." June 28, 1930.

Treml, William. "Neglected Cemetery Resting Spot of County Pioneers." Ann Arbor District Library, via *Ann Arbor News*, August 18, 1976. https://aadl.org/sites/default/files/articles/aa_news_19760818_p25-neglected_cemetery_resting_spot_of_county_pioneers.jpg?fbclid=IwAR1tDlwp2dgOuKXya5TU10SffkzcJkGM0eSzUjBoQTcPnPyVh1kAT5ZdKbI.

Tributes. "Clive Clymer Obituary." https://www.tributes.com/obituary/show/Clive-E.-Clymer-92976332.

Unionville Crescent. "Central Lake Suffers $75,000 High School Fire." February 18, 1927.

UpNorthLive. "Now You Know: The Hauntings at Blue Pelican Inn." YouTube, October 18, 2012. https://www.youtube.com/watch?v=igqytKG7qSI.

Urban, Mark. "7 Years for 7 Monks." *Traverse City Record-Eagle*, September 19, 2018. https://www.record-eagle.com/news/business/7-years-for-7-monks/article_40954e7a-1670-52b2-9a61-956fac119caf.html#:~:text=7%20Monks%20Taproom%20opened%20just%20before%20Labor%20Day.

U.S. Army Corps of Engineers. "Soo Locks History." https://www.lre.usace.army.mil/Missions/Recreation/Soo-Locks-Visitor-Center/Soo-Locks-History.

Weidman Area Centennial Committee. Weidman Area Centennial History Book (1894–1994).

West Side Detroit Polish American Historical Society. "Manya (Abick) Soviak Interview (with Greg Suski and Edward J. Sarna)." August 1, 2007. https://www.detroitpolonia.org/manya-abick-soviak-interview-with-greg-suski-and-edward-j-sarna.

Yale Expositor. "Minor Michigan Matters." May 24, 1901.

ABOUT THE AUTHOR

Nicole Beauchamp is a native of Bay City, Michigan, and received her bachelor's degree in applied science from Siena Heights University in Adrian, Michigan. In addition to being an author, she also works as a licensed massage therapist. With a lifelong passion for the paranormal and history, Nicole founded the Tri-City Ghost Hunters Society (TCGHS) in 2009. Since forming the group, she has investigated all over the world. Over the years, she has presented at various libraries and universities within the state with the goal of educating individuals on the paranormal and expressing the importance of preserving history through investigation. She has had the honor of co-lecturing with renowned paranormal researcher John E.L. Tenney, and her work has been featured in dozens of national and international publications. In 2015, she wrote a guest editorial for *TAPS Paramagazine* and was featured on *Beyond Reality Radio*, where she was recognized for her hard work and dedication to the paranormal by Jason Hawes, the star of the popular television shows *Ghost Nation* and *Ghost Hunters*. In February 2019, she was featured on the cover of *Paranormal Underground* magazine. She received a tribute from the State of Michigan for her first book, *Haunted Bay City, Michigan*, which was released in September 2020. She released her second book, *Haunted Detroit*, in August 2022. In addition to the paranormal, she loves traveling and animals. She hopes to continue to tour Michigan in order to enlighten individuals on the spirit realm.

FREE eBOOK OFFER

Scan the QR code below, enter your e-mail address and get our original Haunted America compilation eBook delivered straight to your inbox for free.

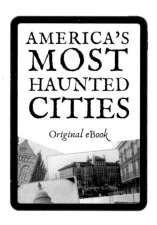

ABOUT THE BOOK

Every city, town, parish, community and school has their own paranormal history. Whether they are spirits caught in the Bardo, ancestors checking on their descendants, restless souls sending a message or simply spectral troublemakers, ghosts have been part of the human tradition from the beginning of time.

In this book, we feature a collection of stories from five of America's most haunted cities: Baltimore, Chicago, Galveston, New Orleans and Washington, D.C.

SCAN TO GET
AMERICA'S MOST HAUNTED CITIES

Having trouble scanning? Go to:
biz.arcadiapublishing.com/americas-most-haunted-cities